THE CAPTAIN'S WIFE

THE
CAPTAIN'S WIFE

The South American Journals of
Maria Graham 1821-23

───────

COMPILED AND EDITED BY

ELIZABETH MAVOR

WEIDENFELD AND NICOLSON
LONDON

Compilation and original editorial matter
copyright © 1993 by Elizabeth Mavor

First published in Great Britain in 1993
by George Weidenfeld and
Nicolson Limited
Orion House
5 Upper St Martin's Lane
London WC2H 9EA

British Library Cataloguing in
Publication Data is available

ISBN 0 297 81296 3

Photoset by Deltatype Ltd,
Ellesmere Port, Cheshire
Printed in Great Britain by
Butler & Tanner Ltd, Frome and London

For Felix Pearson

Contents

Acknowledgements

I should like to thank the Bodleian Library for permission to photograph the printed journals of Maria Graham in their possession, and also the National Portrait Gallery for kind permission to reproduce her portrait.

I am grateful, as ever, to Sybil Cook for her excellent typing and to Rosemary Legge at Weidenfeld for her careful preparation of the manuscript for publication.

Finally I should especially like to thank Sophie Mavor who introduced me to the heroine of these adventures in the first place.

Introduction

Maria Graham is probably better known as Lady Callcott, author of that popular and responsible work, *Little Arthur's History of England*. But it was as Maria Graham, wife of Captain Thomas Graham RN, that she wrote the journals now becoming recognized as giving, among other things, a unique and important insight into the dramatic South American struggle for Independence.

In 1821 Captain Graham and his wife set out for Brazil in the 42-gun frigate *Doris* with orders to keep a godfatherly eye on British trading interests in that unreliable part of the world. By this time the breakaway of the South American provinces from the three-hundred-year-old rule of Portugal and Spain was well advanced, though fraught, as indeed ever since, with difficulty. Nevertheless that New World, soon to be welcomed by George Canning, the British Foreign Secretary, was inexorably coming into being.

Maria Graham understood the historical importance of this development and her country's part in it, and her journals which include excellent concise histories of both Brazil and Chile, feature vivid portraits of the principal actors in the drama. She knew well Don Pedro of Brazil, the liberal Portuguese prince, also Bernardo O'Higgins, the engaging if ambiguous Director of the new Chilean republic. She met, and in spite of herself was impressed by, General San Martin, the enigmatic liberator of Chile and Peru, and she was a dear friend of Lord Cochrane, the Scottish mercenary, who had been invited by the patriots to command the Brazilian and Chilean navies.

She was also to record events at a more local level, as observed in the cobwebbed houses of the slatternly Portuguese gentlewomen of Bahia who entertained in their curlpapers; in the smart new villas of the hard-headed bourgeoisie of the English colony, engrossed, so she tells us, by sugars and cottons to the exclusion of all else but cigars and gambling; in the hovels of the native country people and the black slave markets, people whose lives both appalled and moved her.

'They are ignorant,' she wrote indignantly, 'oppressed, and, perhaps naturally indolent and timid. But the cry of independence has gone forth, the star of freedom has appeared on their horizon . . . never again will the iron sceptre of the Mother Country be stretched out over these lands.'[1]

She was adept at describing such people. When at the age of thirty-six she embarked for Brazil she was already a professional writer, had published a journal of her Indian travels, and another of three months spent with her husband and the painter, Charles Eastlake, in the banditti-riddled mountains east of Rome.

By this journal even the waspish critics of the day had been impressed, finding it '. . . almost a new field of enquiry', chiefly because unlike the usual droning catalogue of Rome and its antiquities, this was concerned exclusively with the lives of Italian peasants and their families.

In its lively pages readers discovered what the Italian peasants liked reading (tales of robbers, miracles, martyrs, but also stories from Tasso and Metastasio); what fun it was to go to a peasant Harvest Home and find yourself spearing dainties from a communal dish with a split stick; how in such circles it was considered impolite to refer to a pig as *porco* (*animale nero* was the correct term) and Maria charmingly described those attractive creatures twinkling along the highway each evening to welcome their masters home from work.

Similar insights were gleaned from the Brazilian and Chileno peasants she encountered as she joined them at their meals (bravely sucking up herbal tea from a communal tube); peered into their hovels to study the sleeping arrangements; drank in their wine shops, made pottery, attended church, rode with them. Her sketches as well as her pen evoked their world, its landscapes, its creatures and flowers with an observation as accurate and sensitive as that of Charles Darwin visiting the same regions ten years later, so that anyone who wants to know how that world then was, in all its exoticism and wonderful beauty, has only to consult her pages.

Although she affected to find journalizing 'a kind of substitute for reading new books of the day',[2] something not so easy in the wilder parts of South America, she took it extremely seriously.

She wrote for at least four hours daily, and often longer, and when she came to prepare her work for publication subjected herself to a set of strict rules. No quoting from private letters. No quoting from private conversations. If she had not personally witnessed the events described she took care to interview living people who had, besides consulting documents of every kind – log

books, gazettes, proclamations, letters, newspapers, official documents – and it is this, coupled with the fact that she made herself
fluent in both Portuguese and Spanish, which gives her work its
peculiar integrity.

The original drafts of her journal remained private however.
What we are permitted to read is what she called a 'copied journal'.
Less characteristic, she herself admitted, but nevertheless equally
true, 'true to nature, true to facts, and true to a better feeling than
often dictates the momentary lines of spleen and suffering . . .'[3]

Those lost lines of spleen and suffering must of course be
regretted by the reader. Yet one has only to open her pages to find
that contrary to her own draconian ethic she frequently airs
prejudices, complains, laughs, and even, though rarely, quotes
from *both* private letters and conversations.

To read Maria Graham is to be more than usually aware of her
private being. Not only of her admirable integrity and loyalty, her
continuing passion for justice (in particular for the poor and
enslaved), but of her relationships: with her much loved and
admired husband Tom; with the young midshipmen of the *Doris*
whom he committed to her care and who in their letters addressed
her as 'my dear Mama'; and with Lord Cochrane. Her friendship
with him was lasting, and based less on the fact that he was a man
and she an attractive woman (she recognized no essential difference between men and women but that of education), than that
they were both fascinated by science – steam engines, printing
presses, copper mills, machinery indeed of all kinds, as well as the
excesses of the natural world around them. It was also important
that Lord Cochrane greatly admired Captain Graham who had
once been his midshipman.

With other women keeping journals at about this time Maria had
much in common. Like Fanny Burney say, or Maria Edgeworth, or
the actress Fanny Kemble, she was well educated, loved books and
travel, of a liberal mind, sharing with Fanny Kemble in particular a
detestation of slavery in all its aspects. Her energy and intellectual
grip put one in mind of Harriet Martineau, and indeed, had she
lived longer, she was certainly destined to have become a reformer
of some kind. Yet her other interests were at the time considered of
a masculine cast, and this tended to prejudice the idea people had
of her. 'Her works I have not read, but I believe they are
unfeminine and abusive,'[4] the 4th Lord Holland wrote.

The impression is in part explained by her being an admiral's
daughter and a naval captain's wife, for whom there was no sea
term with which she was not conversant, no corner of a ship a

mystery. But she was intrigued by many things not necessarily nautical, manufactories, politics, botany, art and what we would now call anthropology, to name only a few.

That she had such interests inevitably invites comparison with her male counterparts who were writing at the same time; Lord Cochrane's interpreter and personal secretary, W. B. Stevenson, whose *Narrative of 20 years residence in South America* came out in 1825, a year after her own journals were published; *Travels in Chile and La Plata* by her friend, John Miers, which was published a year later; Charles Darwin's journal of the countries visited by HMS *Beagle*. With all of these her work in its precision, range and vitality compares favourably, and in her analysis of the problems of the emerging countries of Brazil and Chile she saw all too accurately into the future: the too great dependence on commodities, the racial division between Indian and European, the interference of the Western Powers. What she did not foresee was the devastating exhaustion of the environment.

Yet the critics were to treat the South American journals cantankerously. The reviewer for the *Quarterly* pounced on a misstatement concerning the population of Valparaiso, and wrote triumphantly as an index-heading 'Mrs Graham's inaccuracy proved',[5] going on to criticize her support for Lord Cochrane and to castigate that hero.

'I could forgive any abuse of myself,' she wrote furiously to her publisher, John Murray, 'but I never can forgive injustice to my friends . . .'[6] after which, like the sensible woman she was, she drowned anger in a spate of work.

Maria Graham's *Journal of a Voyage to Brazil*, and *Journal of a Residence in Chile* were published in 1824, and are in both senses great works. For this reason what follows is more in the nature of a selection. In this I have sought to include not only the political aspects of her encounter with South America, but her social life among the colonial Portuguese and Spanish, and among the patriots and native peoples of Brazil and Chile, as well as her own private life as it was lived in the cosy cabin of the *Doris*, and in the temporary homes she so bravely made for herself on those strange and faraway shores.

The following represents perhaps a third of her written work. In the interests of easier reading I have split up some of her monumental paragraphs, smoothed out her scrupulously accurate though taxing punctuation. Otherwise, it is as she wrote it.

1

Beginnings

She was born, the eldest of four children, in 1785 in the small Cumberland market town of Cockermouth, where the poet Wordsworth was later born. Her father, younger son of a cadet branch of the well-known Scottish family of Dundas, had served as a naval officer in the American War of Independence, had come home on half-pay and, perhaps injudiciously, fallen in love and married. His bride, a Miss Thomson, was a young and beautiful loyalist refugee who had fled from America to relations in Liverpool.

Though having to follow their father (now in the Revenue Service) from station to station, the early childhood of the Dundas children was happy if straitened. Maria herself retained particularly happy memories of Wallasey in Cheshire, where the family moved when she was seven, and where she had her own little garden to dig in, and a Highland pony that could be ridden up the garden steps and into the house, and where on winter nights she loved sitting on a stool by her mother's side being told stories from the Bible and Shakespeare.

Poor Mrs Dundas was delicate however, and was soon no longer strong enough to educate her eldest daughter, so to her delight Maria was sent to the local school. There now followed an ecstatically 'uncontrouled' period of her life when Maria helped with the haymaking and sheepshearing on Farmer Hazell's nearby farm, and played hide and seek with Sam Hazell among the vats and cheese presses and once, memorably, recited with Sam the words of the Lord's Prayer backwards in the hope of arousing the Devil.

1

Mrs Dundas growing ever more delicate, Maria's life at Wallasey was abruptly brought to an end on 16 March 1793. Like those fictional heroes David Copperfield and Jane Eyre, she was to be sent immediately away to school.

A rough crossing to Liverpool in a small ferry steered by her father, a three-day coach journey from Liverpool to London broken by a brief stay with fashionable and seemingly unsympathetic cousins at Richmond, was succeeded by a twelve-hour journey in a lumbering yellow coach to Abingdon in Berkshire. Here the exhausted child had a further two miles to walk before reaching her new school at Drayton and being put to bed with tea and bread and butter.

When she awoke next morning her father had already left; she was not to see him nor her brothers and sister for a number of years. Her mother she never saw again. Early on during Maria's schooldays she died of the tuberculosis which also dogged her elder daughter's health.

Although only recently established, the school in the old Manor House at Drayton was to influence the small girl both intellectually and spiritually for life.

It was run by the two Miss Brights, daughters of an impecunious clergyman. The elder Miss Bright had been governess to the daughters of a friend of Dr Johnson, had enjoyed the signal honour of meeting the great man, and through him of becoming an intimate of the Burney family and their circle from whose conversation she had garnered a store of literary anecdotes. She herself was a blue-stocking, vague as to her personal appearance according to her sharp-eyed pupil – hair very unevenly frizzed, cap skewed too far to left or right, pockets absently stuffed with bulky objects which made her look as though she were wearing a hoop. Miss Mary, though lacking her sister's august presence, seems to have been altogether neater and more handsome.

The two sisters were supported in the running of their modest curriculum by two French émigrés, who taught that language; a delicate young man who taught dancing and played the fiddle; and by Dr Crotch, organist at Christ Church who taught the girls music – he who as a tiny child had remarked while on a country walk 'Mother, that cow lows in G.'[1]

Into this genteelly impoverished society erupted the eight-year-old Maria Dundas – a savage, according to her later self – 'Rather little for my age I had black, strait and scanty hair, a white skin and high colour; high-shouldered and awkward in the greatest degree, with very ill-made hands and feet I was full of curiosity, neither very quick nor very slow at learning. I was very good natured, but violent in my temper. [This could be Jane Eyre speaking.] I squabbled with my school-fellows, but they all liked me, and I gave my governess more trouble than any child she ever took in hand; but for all that she loved me better than any of the rest.'[2]

A year later this propensity to violence resulted in an impressive Armageddon between Maria and Miss Bright.

Maria becoming over excited during a game of 'Catch Her' in the garden bites an elder pupil, kind Miss Pasley, on the thumb, and like David Copperfield is made to wear a label with 'Tiger' written upon it. A fortnight later she again bites, this time it's a dreary girl called Miss Pettinger. On being ordered to apologize by poor Miss Mary she refuses, dashing an inkwell to the ground in her rage, and on Miss Mary remonstrating bellows 'I excercise over you the power that strong minds have over weak ones.'[3]

For this she is sent instantly to Coventry by Miss Bright until an apology is forthcoming, and in Coventry she remains 'for months'. During this time no one is permitted to speak to her, she is forbidden to employ herself in any way, is at morning and evening prayers allowed only to kneel outside the schoolroom door to listen but not take part, eats alone, sleeps alone, and for the remainder of the day sits on a box facing the wall in the corner of Miss Bright's parlour.

Here she perforce has to listen to Miss Bright giving the elder girls their lessons. Dull Scripture. Duller History. Then one day she hears Miss Pasley (she of the bitten thumb) reading movingly from the adventures of Aeneas and Dido. When Miss Bright and her pupils file out she looks up from her penitential box and sees opposite, a bookcase, and in it a volume of Pope's *Iliad*, takes it down, lays it in her lap, begins to read. *The Odyssey*, *The Tempest*, various histories both ancient and modern are devoured, she never realizing that as she reads them these books are being secretly replenished by Miss Bright. The holidays arrive. 'I was too fierce to be sent amongst my uncle's gentle children, so there I sat upon my box, and nobody left in the house but dull, unhappy Charlotte G., who had no home to go to!'[4]

It was now that clever Miss Bright somehow contrived a suitable opening for repentance, instantly seized upon by her once obstinate pupil, with the happy result that, 'The third night of the holidays, which had begun so sadly, found me sitting at tea with my kind friends, Miss Mary's favourite cat on my knee.'[5]

She never looked back. Nine years later she left Drayton, in Miss Bright's eyes at any rate, a star pupil. For although her self-confessed plainness of person and want of fashion in her address was unchanged, and she still couldn't or wouldn't dance, she was furnished in other ways, speaking fluent French, able to draw, interested in botany, philosophy, metaphysics, and able, moreover, to hold her own in conversation with those Oxford luminaries to whom Miss Bright had so proudly introduced her; the Dean of Christ Church, the Professor of Hebrew, the botanically minded Dr Barrington. For it was at Drayton that she acquired a taste for the company of clever men, and it was surely at Drayton that she learned those 'daily and hourly imitations of Christ',[6] practised by her governess with a simplicity and humility Maria never forgot.

She was now at ease in society, considered quite civilized enough to stay with her Dundas uncle and fashionable cousins at Richmond, and to enjoy the company of the cultivated French émigrés and other foreigners who thronged the house; the Marquis Lally de Tolendal, who had escaped from France on the eve of the September massacres, Count Woronzow, the Russian Ambassador, Prince Starhemberg, the Vienna Envoy, the French King, Louis Philippe. Through the Miss Berrys, cousins of her father, she was to meet Horace Walpole, visiting his delicious extravaganza at Strawberry Hill 'till I knew its contents by heart, could fancy the picture stepping out of its frame that suggested the famous scene in *The Castle of Otranto*, admired the ancient portraits of Holbein and others, and was too great a novice in antiquarian matters to be able to separate the worthless nick-nacs from the really curious things with which Strawberry Hill abounded.'[7] And when Walpole's niece, Mrs Damer, succeeded to Strawberry, she visited that lady's studio in the garden to watch the good-natured but highly unfeminine sculptress energetically 'spoiling marble'.

The most enjoyable visit of her youth, however, was to Edinburgh, that capital where young ladies, it was said, talked metaphysics as they set to their partners in the reels. United for the first time in years with her father and brothers and sister, Maria chose to ignore the reels and plunged into conversation, with Dugald Stewart, Professor of Moral Philosophy, John Playfair, Professor of Mathematics, and it was not long before she was known, to her secret delight, as 'Metaphysics in Muslin'.

It was now, at the age of twenty, and at the height of enjoyment, that the tuberculosis, clearly inherited from her mother, first showed itself. She fell ill, was for a long period convalescent, and for even longer was unable to regain her strength. Nevertheless, two years later, this strange grave girl, who had claimed she was 'not likely to trouble love either in the abstract or in any other way',[8] her beaux being either over fifty or small schoolboy cousins, had surprisingly fallen in love.

Towards the end of 1808 Maria, now twenty-three, set out for Bombay where her father had been appointed Commissioner for the Navy. He no doubt had it in mind for his daughters to find suitably rich husbands among the gentlemen of the English colony. If so, he hoped in vain, for travelling out as a passenger on their ship was a Lieutenant Tom Graham, scion of a well-known Scottish family.

During the five-months-long voyage Maria, who kept to a scrupulous daily timetable, usefully divided her time teaching English to the midshipmen of the frigate, learning Persian with another of the ship's officers and discussing Sir Walter Scott's *Marmion* as they rounded the Cape, but it was on Lieutenant Tom Graham that her heart soon became fixed.

By April they were finishing Tacitus together and beginning Stewart's *Philosophy of the Human Mind*. 'G[raham]'s mind is clear and comprehensive,' she wrote, 'with a gentle modesty not often to be met with.'[9] Then on Tuesday 4 May, while just off Madagascar '. . . we pledged our faith to each other . . . and we spoke, not to say we loved, or to convince each other of a passion that we had long mutually understood, but to promise to live for each other . . . But no pen,' she continued, 'can describe the sensations that crowded on my heart as he whispered to me the delight he anticipated in being the father of my children.'[10]

There were difficulties. Her father had certainly hoped for someone richer, for when they reached Bombay three weeks later, a Captain Hay called to pay his addresses to Maria. Fortunately news of her engagement to Tom Graham had already circulated among the English colony, 'which prevented his odious addresses, which I am but too well assured my father would approve'.[11]

Not long after Tom had to leave to join his ship at Madras, and Maria was left desolate, 'finding in study the only relief from the pangs of absence and the discomfort of sickness'.[12] During this time, in the hours she was not writing passionate letters to Tom, she had the Kazi Shihab-ud-dien visit to teach her Persian and read the poet Hafiz with her. She was already making translations of the poems of Firdausi and growing ever more ambitious. 'Shall I ever acquire the Sanscrit . . .' she wistfully asked.

By November she appears to have recovered sufficiently to join a party of friends to explore the rock carvings on the island of Elephanta, though reading between the lines, it seems probable that her father, the Admiral, blenching at the idea of engaging with his strong-minded daughter, had capitulated and agreed to her marriage with Tom Graham, since this took place on 9 December 1809.

The next two years they lived on and off together, in Ceylon, in Madras, in Calcutta, as Tom, commanding first the *Hecate*, and latterly the *Eclipse* was on active service against the French in the Bay of Bengal.

Yet although Maria, as a matter of form, attended the balls, masquerades and dinner parties given by the English colony in Calcutta and Madras, it is clear she greatly preferred studying the works of Confucius, learning the Chinese alphabet, drawing antiquities, noting native customs and studying plant and animal life. As regards this an expedition into the jungle to witness the capture of wild elephants particularly moved her. 'I never saw grief and indignation so passionately expressed as by one of these creatures; he groaned, tried to tear his legs from their fetters, buried his trunk in the earth and threw dust into the air. Not even the choicest food, the plantain tree, or the leaf of the young palm could tempt him to eat, or to forget his captivity for many hours. . . .'[13]

At the end of December 1810 a summons came from Tom to return to England as soon as possible since his new command, the *Africaine* (presumably a French prize) had been ordered home. Characteristically before she left Maria found time for an expedition to the ancient town of Maliaballipooram, its wonderful ruined temples and rock carvings overgrown by jungle, half-buried in sand. It must have been one of the last of such expeditions, for by 4 February she was on board the frigate *Barbadoes* bound for home. Four months later her quick ear heard the officer of the watch calling the Captain that the St Agnes lights in Scilly were in sight. 'I have not slept since . . . I can hardly keep my eyes off the land. You do not know what it is to see one's own seas and fields and rocks again. I seem to know every little boat I meet. . . .'[14]

For the next three years she led a literary London life. Her first book, *Journal of a short Residence in India*, came out in 1812, and was well received. But it wasn't long before she was back in Edinburgh. 'She is writing again,' Lady Romilly wrote to the novelist Maria Edgeworth, 'I am sorry to say on heathen Mythology.' She added that the Admiral had died, leaving Maria £5,000 and £100 a year, 'so that they will be comfortable as to money matters'.[15]

The legacy was timely, for with the end of the French wars Tom had been put on half-pay, he and Maria living a mildly resentful

Wordsworthian existence in a cottage at Broughty Ferry with 'two women, two dogs and some poultry'.[16] Maria nevertheless was assiduous in entertaining the rather over-numerous Scottish kinsmen living in the vicinity, studying Latin grammar and Icelandic in her spare time as well as staying up till two in the morning making black puddings.

But the harsh east coast climate didn't suit her, and it wasn't long before she was once more laid up with the familiar feverish cough, only able to console herself with light reading. This time it was Jane Austen's *Emma*, '. . . not that I think it equal to *Pride and Prejudice*, but it quite belongs to that class of innocent and lively novels in which the authoress particularly excels'.[17]

They were back in London again by the beginning of 1817. Dated sketches made during this time reveal that she returned once more to Scotland, but in autumn 1818 was on board HMS *Ganymede* on her way to Italy, making drawings through the stern window – Gibraltar, Malta, Syracuse, Naples, which they reached in December.

They spent almost a year in Italy during which Maria and Tom took three months off with Charles Eastlake, the painter, to stay in one of the mountain villages near Tivoli east of Rome. Aqueducts, olive trees, silkworms, a murdered corpse in a ditch, the broken water gardens of Catena, wild boar . . . Maria indefatigably set herself to study peasant life, while Charles Eastlake drew them and the picturesque *banditti* with which the mountains were infested.

By November 1820 they were again back in England living with friends at Plymouth preparatory to finding a house of their own, but the following spring Tom heard he at last had a command. This was HMS *Doris*, a 42-gun frigate under orders to patrol the coast of Brazil with the object of safeguarding British trading interests. They might well be away three years.

As the Captain's wife Maria was soon immersed in preparations for the voyage, her 'head in a whirl over geese, ducks and fowls, and up to the ears in pickles and preserves'.[18] In the event the *Doris* was prevented from sailing by one tedious delay after another; a court martial, an order (later countermanded) to go to Ireland with the King, a midshipman recalled at the last minute to hold the King's train at the coronation, violent gales . . .

The country to which they were being sent was generally little known, '. . . we have little precise knowledge of Brazil,' a popular historian had written in 1810, 'still less of the interior country of Amazonia'.[19] Unsurprisingly Maria had already taken the trouble to inform herself by reading Von Humboldt's account of his South

American expedition published in 1814, as well as Robert Southey's ample *History of Brazil*.

Brazil's three-hundred-year-old connection with the Portuguese Mother Country was by now drawing to a close. Numerous influences had contributed to this coming separation; the difficulty of running a colony from across the Atlantic, the emboldening example of the revolt from England by the American colonies, the heady ideas of the European Enlightenment, had all played their part in encouraging Brazil to seek her own independence.

As so often it was Napoleon who brought matters to a head. In 1807 the invading French army had reached Lisbon, whereupon, like the King and Queen of Naples before them, the Portuguese royal family had sought the protection of the Royal Navy and removed their court to their colony of Brazil.

The presence of the court at Rio was to transform accepted thinking. For a time Brazil became a kingdom, potentially richer and more powerful than its own mother country. But by 1821 the French menace had for some time been eradicated, and the Portuguese King was preparing to leave for the old country once more. He embarked for Lisbon, taking with him an inordinate amount of treasure, and leaving behind his son, Prince Don Pedro, and the profoundest confusion; contention between the Brazilian provinces, clashes between loyalist Portuguese and native-born Brazilians, and, worst of all, fears that Portugal would once again reduce Brazil to the state of a mere colonial possession.

The King left on 24 April. The Grahams in the *Doris* left the English Channel four months later.

2

Brazil Journal

11 August – 21 September 1821

At about six o'clock in the evening of the 31st of July, 1821, after having saluted His Majesty, George IV, who at that moment went on board the *Royal George* yacht, to proceed to Dublin, – we sailed in the *Doris*, a 42 gun frigate, for South America.

After touching at Plymouth, and revisiting all the wonders of the break-water and new watering place, we sailed afresh, but when off Ushant, were driven back to Falmouth by a heavy gale of wind. There we remained till the 11th of August, when, with colours half-mast high, on account of the death of Queen Caroline, we finally left the channel, and on the 18th about noon came in sight of Porto Santo. . . .

When we passed Porto Santo, and the Desertas, and anchored in Funchal roads, I was disappointed at the calmness of my own feelings, looking at these distant islands with as little emotion as if I had passed a headland in the channel. Well do I remember, when I first saw Funchal twelve years ago, the joyous eagerness with which I feasted my eyes upon the first foreign country I had ever approached, the curiosity to see every stone and tree of the new land, which kept my spirits in a kind of happy fever. . . .

Now I look on them tamely, or at best only as parts of the lovely landscape, which, just at sunset, the time we anchored, was particularly beautiful.

Surely the few years added to my age have not done this? May I not rather hope, that having seen lands whose monuments are all history, and whose associations are all poetry, I have a higher taste, and more discriminating eye? . . .

Early in the morning of the 19th, we took a large party of

midshipmen on shore to enjoy the young pleasure of walking on a foreign land. . . .

We mounted the boys on mules, and rode up to the little parish church, generally mistaken for a convent, called Nossa Señhora da Monte. My maid and I went in a bad sort of palankeen, though convenient for these roads, which are the worst I have seen; however, the view made up for the difficulty of getting to it. . . .

We spent a very happy day at the hospitable country house of Mr Wardrope, and our cavalcade to the town at night was delightful.

The boys, mounted as before, together with several gentlemen who had joined us at Mr W.'s, enjoyed the novelty of riding home by torch-light, and as we wound down the hill, the voices of the muleteers answering each other, or encouraging their beasts with a kind of rude song, completed the scene.

The evening was fine, and the star-light lovely. We embarked in two shore boats at the custom-house gate, and, after being duly hailed by the guard-boat, a strange machine mounting one old rusty six pound carronade, we reached the ship in very good time. . . .

23rd

We sailed yesterday from Funchal, . . .

At night, I sat a long time on the deck, listening to the sea songs with which the crew beguile the evening watch. Though the humourous songs were applauded sufficiently, yet the plaintive and pathetic seemed the favourites; and the chorus to *The Death of Wolfe* was swelled by many voices. . . .

25th

Nothing can be finer than the approach to Teneriffe, especially on such a day as this, the peak now appearing through the floating clouds, and now entirely veiled by them. . . .

We anchored in forty fathoms water with our chain-cable, as the bottom is very rocky, excepting where a pretty wide river, which, though now dry, rolls a considerable body of water to the sea in the rainy season, has deposited a bed of black mud. There are many rocks in the bay, with from one to three fathoms water, and within them from nine to ten.

The swell constantly setting in is very great, and renders the anchorage uncomfortable.

26th

I went ashore with Mr Dance, the second lieutenant, and two of the young midshipmen, for the purpose of riding to the Villa di Oratava, which is situated where the ancient Guanche capital stood.

We landed at the Puerto di Oratava, several miles from the villa. It is defended by some small batteries, at one of which is the very difficult landing-place, sheltered by a low reef of rocks that runs far out, and occasions a heavy surf. I took my own saddle ashore, and being mounted on a fine mule, we all began our journey towards the hill. The road is rough, but has evidently once been made with some pains, and paved with blocks of porous lava, but the winter rains have long ago destroyed it, and it does not seem to be any body's business to put it in repair. . . .

After a pleasant but hot ride, we arrived at the villa about noon, and went to the house of Señor Don Antonio de Monteverde, who accompanied us to M. Franqui's garden, to see one of the wonders of the island, the famous Dragon Tree.

Humboldt* has celebrated this tree in its vigour. It is now a noble ruin. In July, 1819, one half of its enormous crown fell, the wound is plaistered up, the date of the misfortune marked on it, and as much care is taken of the venerable vegetable as will ensure it for at least another century. I sat down to make a sketch of it . . .

The dragon tree is the slowest of growth among vegetables, it seems also to be slowest in decay. In the 15th century, that of Oratava had attained the height and size which it boasted till 1819.

It may have been in its prime for centuries before, and scarcely less than a thousand years must have elapsed, before it attained its full size. . . .

On our return from the garden to Don Antonio's house, we were most kindly received by his wife and daughter, the latter of whom played a long and difficult piece of music most excellently. It was, however, English, in compliment to us, though we should have preferred some of her own national airs.

After the music, we were conducted to a table spread in the gallery that surrounds the open court in the middle of the house, and covered with fruits, sweetmeats, and wines, which were pressed upon us most hospitably; till finding it time to return, the ladies both embraced me, and we began our journey down the hill, having first looked into the churches, which are spacious and

---

* Alexander von Humboldt (1769–1859), traveller and scientist.

handsome, a good deal in the style of those of Madeira, but finer. . . .

We returned to the port by a longer road than that by which we left it. In the hedges, the boys,* with no small delight, gathered fine ripe black-berries, which were growing among prickly pear and other tropical plants. The fields, vineyards, and orchards we had seen from the former road we now passed through, and as it was a *fiesta*, we saw the peasants in their best attire, and their little mud huts cleanly swept and garnished.

They seem gentle and lively, not much darker than the natives of the south of Europe, and if there be a mixture of Guanche blood, it is said to be traced in the high cheek-bones, narrow chins, and slender hands and feet which in a few districts seem to indicate a different race of men.

I regret that I had not time to see more of the people and the country, but not being travellers from curiosity, and belonging to a service that may not swerve from the strictest obedience, we dared not even think of a farther excursion. . . .

It was sunset before we reached the boats that were to convey us to the ship, and we had some difficulty both in getting off and in going alongside of the frigate, owing to the great swell. The night, however, was fine, and the scene enlivened by the lights in the fishing boats, which, like those in the Mediterranean, are used to attract the fish.

On shore, the lights of the ports and villas, and the fires of the charcoal burners shining from amidst the dark hanging forests of pine, and those of the limekilns in the direction of Laguna, appeared like a brilliant illumination, and there being not a cloud, the outline of the peak was well defined on the deep blue of the nocturnal sky.

28th

This morning left the 'still vext'.† bay of Oratava, and before sunset saw Palma and Gomera. . . .

We brought with us from Oratava one of the finest goats I ever saw. I presume she was a descendant of the original flock which the supreme deity of the Guanches created to be the property of the kings alone. She is brown, with very long twisted horns, a very remarkable white beard, and the largest udder I ever saw.

* The midshipmen of the *Doris*.
† She is adapting from Shakespeare, 'From the still-vexed Bermoothes.'

Sept. 1st

The flying-fish are become very numerous, and whole fleets of medusæ have passed us. Some we have picked up, besides a very beautiful purple sea-snail.

This fish has four horns, like a snail, the shell is very beautifully tinted with purple, and there is a spongy substance attached to the fish which I thought assisted it to swim: it is larger in bulk than the whole fish. One of them gave out fully a quarter of an ounce of purple fluid from the lower part of the fish.

A fine yellow locust and a swallow flew on board, and as we believe ourselves to be four hundred miles from the nearest land, Cape Blanco, we cannot enough admire the structure of the wings that have borne them so far.

Our school for the ship's boys is now fairly established, and does Mr Hyslop, our school-master, great credit. That for the midshipmen is going on very well, being kept in the fore-cabin under the captain's eye. The boys have his presence, not only as a check to idleness or noise, but as an encouragement to industry.

He is most anxious to make them fit to be officers and seamen in their profession, and good men and gentlemen both at sea and on shore. Happily they are all promising, but if G–* should disappoint us, I never will believe in youthful talent, industry, or goodness more.

Our days pass swiftly, because busily. The regular business of the ship, the school, astronomical observations, study of history and modern languages, and nothing permitted to pass without observation, fill our time completely.

The books we intend our boys to read are, – history, particularly that of *Greece, Rome, England*, and *France*. An outline of general history, voyages, and discoveries. Some poetry, and general literature, in French and English. Delolme, with the concluding chapter of Blackstone on the history of the law and the constitution of England, and afterwards the first volume of Blackstone, Bacon's *Essays*, and Paley.

We have only three years to work in, and as the *business* of their life is to learn their profession, including mathematics, algebra, nautical astronomy, theory and practice of seamanship, and duty as officers, with all the *technicalities* belonging to it, – this is all we dare propose.

---

* Probably J. D. Glennie, a passed midshipman on the *Doris*, and Maria's cousin.

5th

We have begun to look forward to that festival of the seamen, the crossing the line. I know not whence the custom is derived, but the Arabs observe it with ceremonies not very unlike those practised by our own sailors.

To-day a letter, containing a sketch of the intended festival, with thanks for permission to keep it, was sent into the cabin. I shall copy it with its answer.

I find that some captains have begun to give money at the next port, instead of permitting this day of misrule. Perhaps they may be right, and perhaps in time it may be forgotten; but will it be better that it should be so? It is the sailors' only festival; and I like a festival: it gives the heart room to play. . . . But to our letters.

> *The sons of Neptune, of His Majesty's ship* Doris, *commanded by Captain T.G., return their most grateful thanks for his kind condescension for granting them the favour that has been allowed to them from time immemorial, in crossing the Equinoctial, on our Old Father Neptune's dominions, when we hope the characters will meet your Honour's approbation, which will appear in the margin.*

Thomas Clark, quarter-master,	– *Neptune.*
J. Ware, forecastle,	– *Amphitrite.*
W. Knight,	– *Amphitrite's Son.*
W. Sullivan, 2d captain main-top,	– *Triton.*
C. Brisbane (negro),	– *Triton's Horse.*
J. Thompson, gunner's mate,	– *High Sheriff.*
J. White, forecastle,	– *Sub Sheriff.*
W. Sinclair, captain forecastle,	– *Barber.*
J. Smith, J. Forster, Michael Jaque,	– *Barber's Mates.*
J. Gaggin,	– *Clerk.*
W. Bird, captain fore-top,	– *Chief Constable.*
Nine assistants.	
J. Duncan, boatswain's mate,	– *Coachman.*
J. Clark,	– *Postilion.*
J. Leath,	– *Footman.*
J. Speed,	– *Painter.*
W. Lundy,	– *Bottle-holder.*
W. Williamsom	– *Satan.*
J. Williams,	– *Judge Advocate.*
Eight Sea-horses.	

> *So we have given you as good a relation as possibly our weak abilities afford us; and, hononoured Captain, believe us when we say, we wish you every happiness*

this life can afford, and your honoured lady entirely
included, and believe us yours, &c. &c. &c.

Britton's Sons.

ANSWER.

I received your letter with the list of characters
that are to appear in Father Neptune's train on our
crossing the line, of which I completely approve.
I have to thank you for your kind wishes both for
Mrs G— and myself, and to assure you, that the
greatest pleasure I can feel in the command of this
ship, will be in promoting the happiness and comfort
of the whole of Britain's sons on board the Doris.
Believe me your sincere friend,

Thos. G—,

HMS Doris, *at Sea, Sept. 5th, 1821.*
To Britain's Sons, HMS Doris.

18th

We have done nothing but sail on with very variable weather, for
the last thirteen days. . . . Last night at 8 p.m. we crossed the line.
To-day, accordingly, our Saturnalian festival took place.

About six o'clock p.m. yesterday, the officer of the watch was
informed that there was a boat with lights alongside, and begged to
shorten sail. The captain immediately went on deck, and Neptune
hailed from the fore part of the rigging,

'What ship?'

'Doris.'

'Who commands?'

'Captain T. G.'

'Where from?'

'Whitehall.'

'Where bound?'

'A man of war's cruize.'

Upon which Triton mounted upon a sea-horse, admirably
represented, appeared as bearer of a letter containing the names of
all who had not yet crossed the line, and who were consequently to
be initiated into the mysteries of the Water God.

Triton having thus executed his commission, rode off, and was
seen no more till 8 o'clock this morning, when Neptune being
announced, the captain went on deck to receive him.

First came Triton mounted as before, then a company of sea-
gods or constables dressed in oakum and swabs, but having their

15

arms and shoulders bare, excepting the paint which bedaubed them.

Neptune with trident and crown, Amphitrite by his side, and their son at their feet, appeared in a car drawn by eight sea-horses, and driven by a sea-god. The train followed in the persons of the lawyers, barbers, and painters. The whole pageant was well dressed, and going in procession, fully as picturesque as any antique triumphal or religious ceremony.

The fine forms of some of the actors struck me exceedingly. I never saw marble more beautiful than some of the backs and shoulders displayed, and the singular clothing to imitate fishes instead of legs, and seaweed skirts, which they had all adopted, carried one back for centuries, to the time when all this was religion.

After the progress round the decks, a conference with the captain, and a libation in the form of a glass of brandy, to which the god and goddess vied with each other in devotion, the merriment began.

Mock-shaving, or a fine paid, was necessary to admit the new comers to the good graces of their watery father. And while he was superintending the business, all the rest of the ship's company, officers and all, proceeded to duck each other unmercifully. None but women escaped, and that only by staying in my cabin.

The officer of the watch, sentries, quartermasters, and such as are absolutely necessary to look after the ship, are of course held sacred, so that some order is still preserved. It seemed really that 'madness ruled the hour', but at the appointed moment, half past eleven, all ceased. By noon, everybody was at his duty, the decks were dried, and the ship restored to her wonted good order.

The whole of our gunroom officers dine with us, and we flatter ourselves that we shall end the day as happily as we have begun it.

Friday, September 21st

At length we are in sight of the coast of Brazil, which here is low and green, about two degrees to the northward of the point first discovered by Vincente Pinzon, in 1500.

The weather is very squally, and there is a heavy swell. We are anchored about eight miles from Olinda, the capital of Pernambuco, in fifteen fathoms water, but though we have fired more than one gun for a pilot, none seems to be coming off.

22 September – 13 October 1821

Pernambuco, September 22 1821

At nine o'clock the commodore of this place, whose office is a combination of port-admiral and commissioner, came on board with the harbour-master, and the ship was guided by the latter to the anchorage, which is about three miles from the town, in eight fathoms water. The roadstead is quite open, and we find here a very heavy swell.

It is not wonderful that our guns were neither answered nor noticed last night. Mr Dance, having been sent on shore with official letters to the governor and the acting English consul, found the place in a state of siege, and brought back with him Colonel Patronhe, the governor's aide-de-camp. . . .

From the Colonel they learned that Brazilian rebels had attacked the town during the night, but had been beaten back by the royalist troops under Luis do Rego, the Portuguese governor.

The Colonel gave them to understand that three weeks before, the rebels, or 'patriots' as they called themselves, had declared do Rego's government at an end, and immediately elected a rival one of their own. This with 'that disposition to revolution, which we were aware had long existed in every part of Brazil . . .' commented Maria dryly.

Meanwhile, having discovered unwelcome nests of armed patriots concealed in a number of the town belfreys, the Pernambucans were in a state of high alert . . .

The towns-people have been formed into a militia, tolerably armed and trained. The town is pretty well supplied with mandioc flour, jerked beef,* and salt fish, but the besiegers prevent all fresh provisions from coming in. All shops are shut, and all food scarce and dear.

Most people who have property of value, in plate or jewels, have packed it up, and lodged it in the houses of the English merchants. Many persons with their wives and families have left their homes in the outskirts of the town, and have taken refuge with the English. The latter, who, for the most part, sleep, at least, in country houses in the neighbourhood, called *sitios*, have left them,

---

* Slices of beef dried in the sun.

and remain altogether at their counting-houses in the port. Everything, in short, is alarm and uncertainty.

23rd

The night passed quietly, and so indeed did the day. Many messages have passed between us and the land, but I could not go on shore. We have excellent oranges, and tolerable vegetables from the town, and have been quite enough amused in observing the curious little boats, canoes, catamarans and jangadas, that have been sailing, and paddling, and rowing round the ship. . . .

Monday, the 24th

Col. Patronhe arrived early this morning, to request that the English packet might put into Lisbon with the Government despatches.

We felt glad that the strict rules of service prevented the captain from giving any such order to the master of the packet. It would be at once a breach of that neutrality we profess to observe, and, in my opinion, an aiding of the worst cause.* The colonel, adverting to the town being in a state of siege, and the uncertainty of the next attack as to time and place, advised me strongly to stay altogether on board, but I had never seen a town in a state of siege, and therefore resolved to go ashore. Accordingly, Mr Dance being the only officer on board who speaks either Portuguese or French, was commissioned to accompany me, and I took two midshipmen, Grey and Langford, also to call on Madame do Rego.† . . . We rowed up the harbour among vessels of all nations, with the town on one side, and the reef on the other, until we came to one of the wide creeks, over which the Dutch built a fine stone bridge, now in decay.

We were a good deal struck with the beauty of the scene. The buildings are pretty large, and white; the land low and sandy, spotted with bright green tufts of grass, and adorned with palm-trees. . . . We landed pretty near the bridge, and were received by Colonel Patronhe, who apologized for the governor, who could not come to receive us, as he was in the council room.

The colonel conducted us to the government house, a very handsome building, with a square in front, and a tower, and we entered what had evidently been a splendid hall.

* The pro-Portuguese party, who were against Brazilian Independence.
† The wife of the governor of Pernambuco.

The gilding and painting still remained on some parts of the ceiling and walls, but now it is occupied by horses standing ready saddled, soldiers armed, and ready to mount at a moment's warning. Every thing on the alert. Guns in front with lighted matches by them, and an air of bustle and importance among the soldiers, that excites a sort of sympathetic curiosity as to their possible and immediate destination.

On going up stairs we found almost as much confusion. For the governor has hitherto lived in the very out-skirts of the town, and has but just come to the house in Sant Antonio, which was formerly the Jesuits' college, partly to be in the centre of business, and partly to secure his family, in case of accident, as the besiegers' out-posts are very near his former residence.

I found Madame do Rego an agreeable, rather pretty woman, and speaking English like a native. For this she accounted, by informing me that her mother, the Viscondeca do Rio Seco, was an Irish woman. Nothing could be kinder and more flattering than her manner, and that of General do Rego's two daughters, whose air and manner are those of really well-bred women, and one of them is very handsome.

After sitting some little time, refreshments were brought in, and shortly after, the governor himself appeared, a fine military-looking man. He appeared ill, being still suffering from the effects of a wound he received some months ago, while walking through the town with a friend. It has since been ascertained, that the instigator of the crime was a certain Ouvidor (judge) whom he had displaced shortly after he assumed government.

The assassin fired twice, Luiz do Rego received several shots and slugs in his body, but the most severe wound was in his left arm. His friend's life was for some time despaired of, but both are now nearly well.

At the time the crime was committed, the perpetrator was seized more than once by some of the bye-standers, but as often, a baker's basket was pushed in between him and whoever seized him. He threw away his pistols and escaped.

Having paid our visit, we proceeded to walk about the town. The streets are paved partly with blueish pebbles from the beach, partly with red or grey granite. The houses are three or four stories high, built of a whitish stone, and all are white-washed, with door-posts and window-frames of brown stone.

The ground floor consists of shops, or lodging for the negroes, and stables. The floor above is generally appropriated to counting-houses and ware-rooms, and the dwelling-house still higher, the kitchen being universally at the top, by which means the lower part of the house is kept cool.

I was surprised to find it so possible to walk out without inconvenience from the heat, so near the equator, but the constant sea-breeze, which sets in here every day at ten o'clock, preserves a temperature, under which it is at all times possible to take exercise. The hot time of day is from eight, when the land breeze fails, to ten. . . .

At each end of every street we found a light gun, and at the heads of the bridges two, with lighted matches by them, and at each post we were challenged by the guard. At the end of the stone bridge, at the *ponte dos tres pontes*, next to Recife, the guards are more numerous and strict.

In this quarter, the chief riches of the place are lodged, and that is the point most easily defended. It is very nearly surrounded with water, the houses are high, strongly built, and close together, the streets being very narrow, and the strong gateways at each end of the bridge might secure time to demolish it entirely, and thus render that part of the town secure, except by the sand bank communicating with Olinda, and that is guarded by two considerable forts.

We had hardly gone fifty paces into Recife, when we were absolutely sickened by the first sight of a slave-market. It was the first time either the boys or I had been in a slave-country. And, however strong and poignant the feelings may be at home, when imagination pictures slavery, they are nothing compared to the staggering sight of a slave-market.

It was thinly stocked, owing to the circumstances of the town, which cause most of the owners of new slaves to keep them closely shut up in the depots. Yet about fifty young creatures, boys and girls, with all the appearance of disease and famine consequent upon scanty food and long confinement in unwholesome places, were sitting and lying about among the filthiest animals in the streets.

The sight sent us home to the ship with the heartache, and resolution, 'not loud but deep', that nothing in our power should be considered too little, or too great, that can tend to abolish or to alleviate slavery.

27th

I went on shore to-day to spend a few days with Miss Stewart, the only English lady in the town. She is now living in her brother's town-house, where the office and warehouses are, because the country-house is within reach of the patriots.* . . .

In the evening we rode out. Whether it was because we had been so many weeks on board ship, and without horse-exercise, or because of the peculiar sweetness and freshness of evening after the sultry tropical day we had just passed, I know not, but I never enjoyed an hour in the open air so much.

We rode out of the town by some pretty country-houses, called *sitios*, to one of the outposts at Mondego, which was formerly the governor's residence. The tamarind, the silk-cotton tree, and the palm, shaded us, and a thousand elegant shrubs adorned the garden walls. It is impossible to describe the fresh delicious feel of such an evening, giving repose and health after the fiery day. We were very sorry when obliged to return home, but the sun was gone, there was no moon, and we were afraid that the guards at the various posts of defence might stop us.

As we came back, we were challenged at every station; but the words, *amigos ingresos* were our passport, and we got to Recife just as the evening hymn was singing, harshly and unmusically enough, by the negroes and mulattoes in the streets. But yet everything that unites men in one common sentiment is interesting. The church doors were open, the altars illuminated, and the very slave felt that he was addressing the same Deity, by the same privilege with his master. It is an evening I can never forget.

28th

This morning before breakfast, looking from the balcony of Mr S[tewart]'s house, I saw a white woman, or rather fiend, beating a young negress, and twisting her arms cruelly while the poor creature screamed in agony, till our gentlemen interfered. Good God! that such a traffic, such a practice as that of slavery, should exist.

Near the house there are two or three depots of slaves, all young. In one, I saw an infant of about two years old, for sale. Provisions are now so scarce that no bit of animal food ever seasons the paste of mandioc flour, which is the sustenance of slaves, and even of this, these poor children, by their projecting bones and hollow cheeks, show that they seldom get a sufficiency.

Now, money also is so scarce, that a purchaser is not easily found, and one pang is added to slavery, the unavailing wish of

* The pro-Independence Brazilians.

finding a master! Scores of these poor creatures are seen at different corners of the streets, in all the listlessness of despair – and if an infant attempts to crawl from among them, in search of infantile amusement, a look of pity is all the sympathy he excites.

Are the patriots wrong? They have put arms into the hands of the *new* negroes, while the recollection of their own country, and of the slave-ship, and of the slave-market, is fresh in their memory.

I walked to-day to the market-place, where there is but little – beef scarce and dear, no mutton, a little poultry, and a few pigs, disgusting, because they feed in the streets where every thing is thrown, and where they and the dogs are the only scavengers.

The blockade is so strict, that even the vegetables from the gentlemen's private gardens, two miles from the out-posts, are detained. No milk is to be had, bread of American flour is at least twice as dear as in England, and the cakes of mandioc baked with cocoa nut juice, too dear for the common people to afford a sufficiency even of them. . . .

Yesterday the motley head-dresses of the Portuguese inhabitants were seen to great advantage, in a sally through the streets, made by a kind of supplementary militia to enforce the closing of all shop-doors, and the shutting up of all slaves, on an alarm that the enemy was attacking the town to the southward.

The officer leading the party was indeed dressed *en militaire*, with a drawn sword in one hand, and a pistol in the other. Then followed a company that Falstaff would hardly have enlisted, armed in a suitable manner, with such caps and hats as became the variety of trades to which the wearers belonged, the rear being brought up by a most singular figure, with a small drum-shaped black cap on the very top of a stiff pale head, a long oil-skin cloak, and in his left hand a huge Toledo, ready drawn, which he carried upright.

The militia are better dressed, and are now employed in regular turn of duty with the royal troops, who are going over to the patriots daily.

Calling at the palace this forenoon, we learned that a hundred Indians are expected in the town, by way of assistance to the garrison. They wear their aboriginal dress, and are armed with slings, bows, and arrows. We are told their ideas of government consist in believing that implicit obedience is due both to king and priests. Brandy is the bribe for which they will do any thing, a dram of that liquor and a handful of mandioc flour being all the food they require when they come down to the port.

This evening, as there are no horses to be hired here, we

borrowed some from our English and French friends, and rode to Olinda by the long sandy isthmus, which connects it with Recife. . . .

The sun was low, long before we reached even the first of the two castles on our way back to the fort. The dogs had already begun their work of abomination. I saw one drag the arm of a negro from beneath the few inches of sand, which his master had caused to be thrown over his remains. It is on this beach that the measure of the insults dealt to the poor negroes is filled.

When the negro dies, his fellow-slaves lay him on a plank, carry him to the beach, where beneath high-water mark they hoe a little sand over him. But to the new negro even this mark of humanity is denied. He is tied to a pole, carried out in the evening and dropped upon the beach, where it is just possible the surf may bear him away. These things sent us home sad and spiritless, notwithstanding the agreeable scenes we had been riding among. . . .

30th

Last night the patriot troops attacked the line of defence at Olinda for four hours, but I do not believe there was any loss on either side. This morning a Portuguese frigate, the *Don Pedro*, with troops from Bahia, arrived. The reinforcement of three hundred and fifty men, partly European, partly Bahian, has put the inhabitants, from the governor downwards, into the highest spirits, so that for once we see Pernambuco active, and cheerful, and alive. Men and women are out in their gayest habits, and the military are running and riding in all directions, not a little pleased to have some to relieve them in their constant watch and ward. . . .

This day several of the officers and midshipmen of the *Doris* accompanied us to dine at the governor's, at half-past four o'clock.

Our welcome was most cordial. His Excellency took one end of the table, and an aide-de-camp the other. I was seated between M. and Madame do Rego. He seemed happy to talk of his old English friends of the Peninsula, with many of whom I am acquainted, and she had a thousand enquiries to make about England, whither she is very anxious to go. They apologized for having so little plate, but their handsome services were packed up in an English storehouse, together with Her Excellency's jewels and other precious things.

The cookery was a mixture of Portuguese and French. After the soup, a dish was handed round of boiled lean beef, slices of fat salt pork, and sausages, and with this dish, rice boiled with oil and sweet herbs. Roast beef was presented, in compliment to the English, very little roasted. Salads, and fish of various kinds, were dressed in a peculiar manner, poultry and other things in the French fashion.

The dessert was served on another table. Besides our European dessert of fruit, cakes, and wine, all the puddings, pies, and tarts, formed part of it. It was decorated with flowers, and there was a profusion of sugar-plums of every kind.

The company rose from the dining-table, and adjourned to the other, which Madame do Rego told me should have been spread in a separate apartment, but they have so recently taken possession of their house, that they have not one yet fitted up for the purpose.

The governor and his guests proposed many toasts alternately – the King of England, the King of Portugal, the navy of England, the King of France, Luis do Rego, and the captaincy of Pernambuco, &c.

When we all rose at once from table, some of the company went on board ship, but most adjourned to the drawing-room, a comfortable apartment, furnished with blue satin damask, where we were joined by the French naval officers of His Most Christian Majesty's ship *Sappho*, and several ladies and gentlemen of the city.

We had some excellent music. Madame do Rego has an admirable voice, and there were several good singers and players on the piano. It was a more pleasant, polished evening than I had expected to pass in Pernambuco, especially now in a state of siege.

Wednesday, 3d October

I went on board on Monday, and, provokingly enough, the patriots chose that very night to make an attack upon the out-post of the Affogadas, so I did not see the governor, at the head of his troops, march out to meet them, nor did I hear the national hymn sung by the regiments as they filed along on their return from a successful sally.

Yesterday, nothing occurred worth noting, we had the consul and British merchants on board to dinner, and the day passed as such days usually do.

Having learned that the patriots have refused to allow the linen belonging to the ship, which had been sent to the country to be washed, to return to the town, it was determined that we should send to their head-quarters, and remonstrate against this very inconvenient mode of annoying the port. I obtained leave to accompany the messengers, and accordingly we all went on shore immediately after breakfast.

Our first business was to procure passports, and to learn the countersigns, after which Capt. Graham, with Col. Cottar, the governor's principal aide-de-camp, rode with us to the out-posts, where we left them, with an intention of returning to dine at Mr Stewart's, to meet Luis do Rego's family.

Our party consisted of M. Caumont, to act as interpreter, Mr Dance, bearing the letter, my cousin Mr Glennie as my cavalier, and myself. It was the first time we had had an opportunity of passing the lines, and we felt like school-boys who had stolen beyond bounds, and well we might. The scenery was fresh and lovely, and the day as fine as possible.

Pernambuco is not a walled town, but broad rapid rivers and æstuaries surround it, and it is only approachable by the roads and causeways. The banks thrown up across these, for present defence, are such as might stop the Brazilian cavalry for a few minutes, or afford covery for musketry, but their best defence is the swamp at the mouth of the Capabaribe, which is flooded at high water, and which extends nearly to the Bibiribi.

At the edge of the swamp there is a wooden palisade, where we left the last post of the royalists, and took leave of our friends, who had accompanied us so far. After riding across the marsh, which by the by is very fit for rice ground, and is surrounded by cocoa-nut and tamarind trees, we came to the main stream of the Capabaribe, a deep, broad, and very rapid river. Its sides are steep, and the water beautifully clear, its banks are studded with country-houses, and adorned with groves and gardens, for the present abandoned by their owners, who have taken refuge in Recife. . . .

About two miles from Do Rego's last out-post, we came to the first post of the patriots, at a country-house on a rising ground, with arms piled at the door, and a sort of ragged guard, consisting of a merry-looking negro with a fowling-piece, a Brazilian with a blunderbuss, and two or three of doubtful colour with sticks, swords, pistols, &c., who told us an officer was to be found.

After a few minutes parley, we found he was not authorized to receive our letter, so we rode on under the direction of the old Brazilian with his blunderbuss, who, being on foot, threatened to shoot us if we attempted to ride faster than he walked.

The slow pace at which we advanced gave us leisure to remark the beauties of a Brazilian spring. Gay plants, with birds still gayer hovering over them, sweet smelling flowers, and ripe oranges and citrons, formed a beautiful fore-ground to the very fine forest-trees that cover the plains, and clothe the sides of the low hills in the neighbourhood of Pernambuco. . . .

After riding a few miles, we came suddenly to the foot of an abrupt hill, on whose sides there were scattered groups of the most magnificent trees I ever beheld. There we were met by a small military party, which, after a parley with our guide, rather ordered, than invited us to ride up. In a few seconds, we came to a steep yellow sandstone bank, shaded on one side by tall trees, and open on the other to a lake surrounded by woody hills, on the most distant of which, the white buildings of Olinda sparkled like snow.

On the top of the bank, and in the act of descending, was a group of forty horsemen, one of the foremost of whom bore a white banner. Several were dressed in splendid military habits, others in the plain costume of the landed proprietors. These were deputies from Paraiba on their way to propose terms to Luis do Rego. They had just left the head-quarters of the besieging army, where the provisional government of Goyana is stationed, and were accompanied by a guard of honour. After exchanging civilities, part of the guard turned back with us, and the deputies went on their way. Having reached the top of the hill, we found about a hundred men, tolerably well armed, but strangely dressed, awaiting us, and there we were detained till our guide rode forward to ask leave to bring us to head-quarters. . . . Our guide soon returned with eighteen or twenty mounted soldiers, whose appearance was rather wild than military. The guard presented arms as we parted from them, and we soon cantered down the hill towards the main body of the troops. Not above two hundred had the arms or accoutrements of soldiers, but there were dresses and weapons of every kind, leather, cloth, and linen, short jackets and long Scotch plaids, and every tint of colour in their faces, from the sallow European to the ebony African. Military honours were paid us by these ragged regiments, and we were conducted to the palace square, where Mr Dance and M. Caumont dismounted, and I determined to await the issue of their conference, with my cousin in the court.

This, however, was not permitted. In a few minutes, a smart little man, speaking tolerable French, came and told me the *government* desired my company.

I suspected a mistake of the word government for governor, and endeavoured to decline the honour, but no denial could be taken, and the little man, who told me he was secretary to government, accordingly assisted me to dismount, and showed me the way to the palace.

The hall was filled with men and horses, like a barrack stable, excepting a corner which served as an hospital for those wounded in the late skirmishes, the groans of the latter mingling uncouthly with the soldiers cheerful noisy voices. The stalls were so crowded, that we got up with difficulty, and then I found that I was indeed to be confronted with the whole strength of the provisional government.

At the end of a long dirty room, that had once been handsome, as the form of the windows and carving of the panels on which there were traces of colour and gilding, indicated, there was an old black hair sofa, on the centre of which I was placed, with Mr Dance on one side, and Mr Glennie on the other. By Mr Dance sat the little secretary, and next to him our interpreter, in old-fashioned high-backed chairs. The rest of the furniture of the room consisted of nine seats of different sizes and forms, placed in a semicircle fronting the sofa, and on each of these sat one of the members of the junta* of the provisional government, who act the part of senators or generals, as the occasion may require.

To each of these I was introduced, the names of Albuquerque, Cavalcante, and Broderod, struck me, but I heard imperfectly, and forget most of them. Some wore handsome military coats, others the humbler dress of farmers. They politely told me they would not read the letter while I was waiting below, but as soon as we were seated, the secretary read it aloud.

Instead of taking any notice of its contents, the secretary began a long discourse, setting forth the injustice of the Portuguese governor and government towards Brazil in general, and the Pernambucans in particular; that in order to resist that injustice, they had formed the present respectable government, pointing to the junta, without intending the least detriment to the rights of the King. That surely they could not be called rebels, as they marched under the royal flag of Portugal, but Luis do Rego might be reasonably stigmatized as such, for he had fired on that banner. . . . We then talked a great deal in French to the secretary, who repeated every word to the respectable junta, and at length got him to attend to a proposal for releasing our linen, and another for supplying the ship with fresh provisions.

We had been paying forty dollars per bullock in the town. They agreed that their price should not exceed ten, if we sent boats to the Rio Doce, or Paratije for them. This is the mouth of a small stream on the northside of Olinda. And I must not omit to mention, that they offered to allow us to take off fresh provisions for our English or French friends in the town.

The junta was extremely anxious to learn if there was a probability of England's acknowledging the independence of

* Council.

27

Brazil, or if she took part at all in the struggle, and many were the questions, and very variously were they shaped, which the secretary addressed to us on that head.

They are of course violent in their language concerning Luis do Rego, in proportion as he has done his military duty, in keeping them at bay with his handful of men, and like all oppositions they can afford to reason upon general principles, because they have not to feel the hindrances of action, and the jarring of private interests in the disposal and fulfilment of office.

I was sitting opposite to one of the windows of the council-room, and had been remarking for some time, that the sun was getting very low, and, therefore, rose to go, having received a note from the secretary, ordering the officers at their advanced posts to offer no hindrance to the passing of any thing belonging to His British Majesty's frigate, *Doris*. But we were not suffered to depart without a hearty invitation to sup and spend the night, and a stirrup-cup (a huge glass) was brought, and a bottle of wine, with about half as much water, poured into it. It was then handed to me to begin, and all fourteen received it in turn.

By this time the guard was drawn out, the band played the national hymn, to which we all listened bare-headed, and so we mounted among those wild-looking men, in that strange, yet lovely landscape, just as the evening mist began to veil the lower land, and the bright red evening sun to gild the topmost branches of the forest.

Our journey home was much more rapid than our journey out. The evening was cool, and the horses eager to return, but we did not reach Mr S[tewart]'s till two hours after sunset, when we found that, after the party had waited till six o'clock, Captain Graham had insisted on their dining. The governor was uneasy, and offered to send a party of Cacadores in search, as he kindly said, of me, – but this, of course, was refused, the captain assuring His Excellency, that if the patriots detained his lieutenant, he would take him back with his own men, and that as to me, while I was with my two companions, he had not the least fear concerning me. . . .

Thursday, 4th

Received Madame do Rego, one of her daughters, Miss S[tewart], and several gentlemen, on board. Most of the party were sea-sick, from the rolling of the ship, caused by the heavy swell at the anchorage. They were, however, highly charmed with their visit, particularly with the fireworks with which we saluted the ladies (who had never been on board a British frigate before), on their departure.

Friday, 5th

According to the agreement made with the patriot officers, on Wednesday, one launch and the second cutter went to Rio Doce to receive bullocks and other provisions. The officers and men were most kindly received, and returned with many presents of fresh stock and vegetables, which the patriots forced upon them. A military band attended them on landing, and conducted them to the place of meeting with the chiefs.

Messrs Biddle and Glennie, being on shore surveying, near Cabo de Sant Augustin, were detained as prisoners for a few hours, by a patriot detachment. But, as it appeared to be only for the purpose of obtaining money, and done by some subaltern, no notice was taken of it.

Saturday, 6th

The frigate got under weigh to take a cruize, and if possible find a quieter anchorage. Mr Dance with a party went for more provisions, to Rio Doce. The surf at the landing place was so high, that they were obliged to get into canoes, and leave the boats grappled at some distance from the beach. A guard of honour and military band attended them, as on the former day, and they were, moreover, pressed to dine with the commander of the post, which they gladly did. . . .

Monday, 8th

We find to-day, on anchoring, that terms have been entered into with the patriots, by which their deputies are to be in the council, and take an equal share in the administration. On the other hand, they are to withdraw the investing troops, and leave Luis do Rego at the head of the military department, until the arrival of the next despatches from Lisbon. These pacific measures were brought about by the Paraiban deputies whom we met on Wednesday.

Tuesday, 9th

Mr Dance, Mr Glennie, and I, were deputed to take charge of a large party of midshipmen, who had not been able before to take a run on shore, to spend the day on Cocoa-nut Island, which lies a good way up the harbour, and within the reef of Pernambuco.

As we sailed along the rock, we observed that it is covered with echini, polypii, barnacles, limpets, and crusted with white bivalves less than oysters or cockles, yet containing a fish not unlike the latter in appearance, and the former in flavour.

We had not exactly calculated the effect of the tide so far up the harbour as Cocoa-nut Island, consequently we got aground in the outer channel, at a considerable distance from the shore. The sailors pushed me over one flat bank in the gig,* and then carried me to the beach. The midshipmen waded, and the officers and boats with the crew, went in search of a deeper passage, where they might approach with our provisions.

Meantime the boys and I had full leisure to examine the island. It is perfectly flat and covered with white sand, the shore scattered with fragments of shells and coral. . . . The whole island abounds in gay shrubs and gaudy flowers, where the humming-bird, here called the *beja flor* or kiss-flower, with his sapphire wings and ruby crest, hovers continually, and the painted butterflies vie with him and his flowers in tints and beauty.

The very reptiles are beautiful here. The snake and the lizard are singularly so, at least in colour. We found a very large rough caterpillar, each hair or prickle of which is divided into five or six branches, the rings of its body are scarlet, yellow, and brown. The country people believe that it hurts the udders of cows, and prevents their giving milk, if it does not actually suck them. They are therefore very unpopular here, because the whole island that is not garden-ground is pasture, and supplies a great deal of the milk for the market of Recife.

While we were endeavouring to forget our hunger by examining the island, and drinking cocoa-nut juice, and wondering at many an ordinary thing, though new to young untravelled eyes (and such were those of most of the party), our boats were taking a circuitous track. At length at ten o'clock they landed our provisions, when we made a hearty breakfast, sitting on a sail spread under the palm shade.

The elder boys with their guns, then accompanied Mr Dance and the captain of a merchant vessel, who volunteered to act as Cicerone,† to shoot, and the younger ones staid with me to collect flowers, gather vegetables, and with the assistance of the boats' crews, to superintend the preparations for dinner.

* A long light boat.
† Guide.

At four o'clock the sportsmen returned, bringing red-crested woodpeckers, finches of various hues, humming-birds, black and yellow pies, and others of gay plumage and delicate shape, quite new to us all.

A merrier party certainly never met, but the best of the expedition was to come. The tide was now favourable, and we determined to do a spirited thing. Instead of going all the way down the harbour, which would have kept us out beyond the time allowed us, we ran through a passage in the reef called Mother Cary's passage, because few things but the birds think of swimming there.

The merchant-boat went first, our gig next. And as I sat in the stern of the large boat that was to follow, it was beautiful, but something fearful, to see them dash through that boiling surf between the rocks and rise over the wave secure beyond it. Nor was the sensation less mixed when we followed.

There is at all times something triumphant in the sensation of sailing over the waters, but when they are roughened by storms, or rendered fearful by rocks or shoals, the triumph approaches to the sublime. In it there is a secret dread, though not of ocean, and a raising of the soul to him who made the ocean, and gave man mind to master it.

I am not ashamed to own, that as I looked round on my young charges, when Mr Dance whispered 'sit still and say nothing', and then stepping to the bow of the boat called aloud to the helmsman 'steady!' I had a moment, though but a moment, of exquisite anxiety.

But we were through in an instant, and soon alongside of the frigate, where we were praised for doing what few had done before, and having shown the possibility of doing that safely, which at some future time it might be of importance to know could be done at all.

Wednesday, 10th

We went on shore early for the first time since the armistice. The guns are removed from the streets and a few of the shops are re-opened, the negroes are no longer confined within doors, and the priests have reappeared. Their broad hats and ample cloaks give them an importance among the crowd, which now is busy and active, and seemingly intent on redeeming the time lost to trade by the siege.

I was struck by the great preponderance of the black population.

By the last census, the population of Pernambuco, including Olinda was seventy thousand, of which not above one third are white, the rest are mulatto or negro.

The mulattoes are, generally speaking, more active, more industrious, and more lively than either of the other classes. They have amassed great fortunes, in many instances, and are far from being backward in promoting the cause of independence in Brazil.

Few even of the free negroes have become very rich. A free negro, when his shop or garden has repaid his care, by clothing him and his wife each in a handsome black dress, with necklace and armlets for the lady, and knee and shoe buckles of gold, to set off his own silk stockings, seldom toils much more, but is quite contented with daily food.

Many, of all colours, when they can afford to purchase a negro, sit down exempt from further care. They make the negro work for them, or beg for them, and so long as they may eat their bread in quiet, care little how it is obtained.

The European Portuguese, are extremely anxious to avoid intermarriage with born Brazilians, and prefer giving their daughters and fortunes to the meanest clerk of European birth, rather than to the richest and most meritorious Brazilian.

They have become aware of the prodigious inconvenience, if not evil, they have brought on themselves by the importation of Africans, and now no doubt, look forward with dread to the event of a revolution, which will free their slaves from their authority, and, by declaring them all men alike, will authorize them to resent the injuries they have so long and patiently borne.

Thursday, 11th

As every thing seems quietly settled between the royalist and patriot chiefs, we are preparing to take leave of Pernambuco, and it is not without regret, for we have been kindly treated by the Portuguese, and hospitably received by our own countrymen.

We went on shore to provide necessaries and comforts for our farther voyage. Among the latter I bought some excellent sweet-meats,* which are made in the interior, and brought to market in neat little wooden kegs, each containing six or eight pounds. . . .

After I had ended my marketing, I went to call on a Portuguese family, and as it was the first private Portuguese house I had been

* The convents are, generally speaking, the places where the more delicate preserves are made. Those I bought were of Guava, cashew apple, citron, and lime. The cashew particularly good. They go by the general name of *Doce*.

in, I was curious to notice the difference between it and the English houses here.

The building and general disposition of the apartments are the same, and the drawing-room only differed in being better furnished, and with every article English, even to a handsome piano of Broadwood's. But the dining-room was completely foreign, the floor was covered with painted cloth, and the walls hung round with English prints and Chinese pictures, without distinction of subject or size.

At one end of the room was a long table, covered with a glass case, enclosing a large piece of religious wax-work, the whole *præsepia*,* ministering angels, three kings, and all, with moss, artificial flowers, shells and beads, smothered in gauze and tiffany, bespangled with gold and silver, San Antonio and St Christopher being in attendance on the right and left. The rest of the furniture consisted of ordinary chairs and tables, and a kind of beaufet or sideboard.

From the ceiling, nine bird-cages were hanging, each with its little inhabitant; canaries, grey finches with a note almost as fine, and the beautiful widow-bird, were the favourites.

In larger cages in a passage room, there were more parrots and paroquets than I should have thought agreeable in one house, but they are well-bred birds, and seldom scream all together.

We were no sooner seated in the dining-room, than biscuit, cake, wine, and liqueurs, were handed round, the latter in diminutive tumblers. A glass of water was then offered to each, and we were pressed to taste it, as being the very best in Recife. It proceeds from a spring in the garden of the convent of Jerusalem, two miles from town, and the only conduit from that spring leads to the garden of a sister convent here.

From the lady, I learned, that the porous jars for cooling water, that we find here, are all made in the neighbourhood of Bahia, there being no manufactory here, except a few coarse cottons for clothing for the slaves.

The air and manners of the family we visited, though neither English nor French, were perfectly well bred, and the dress pretty much that of civilized Europe, only that the men wore cotton jackets instead of cloth coats, and were without neck-cloths; when they go out of doors, however, they dress like Englishmen. . . .

* Manger.

33

Friday, 12th

The Prince Royal of Portugal's birth-day. There is a levee at the palace. The company bow first to the governor, then to the Prince's picture, which is placed in the middle of the audience-room, to receive its due honours, and then the *beja mano*, or kiss hands, takes place.

The forts and ships saluted, we of course did the same, and the people all dressed and went to mass, as on a holiday.

One thing contributed, however, in no small degree to the enjoyment of the day. The troops,* which lately arrived from Bahia, re-embarked in order to return. Their whole behaviour had been disorderly, and their drunkenness and riot, during the ten days they were here, had quite disgusted the people; while the disposition they manifested to join the patriots, had rendered them but suspicious auxiliaries to the governor.

Saturday, 13th

I took leave of my amiable friends at the palace. Madame do Rego gave me several specimens of amethyst, and the stone called minha nove (like aqua marine), and also a fine piece of gold ore of the province. . . .

The scene at our embarking was very pretty. Our friends went with us to the jetty, and our boats lying in the clear moonshine beneath it, with sailors going up and down preparing for us, the harbour and the shipping doubled by the clear reflection in the still water, heightened and set off the sparkling of the breakers that dashed against the outer fort and lighthouse. Through these we soon made our way and reached the ship, where I have once more taken possession of my cabin, and put it in order for sea. . . .

---

* These were troops supporting the Portuguese colonial party against the patriots.

14 October – 8 December 1821

Sunday, Oct. 14th

We got under weigh after breakfast, and soon lost sight of Pernambuco. All Sunday, Monday, and Tuesday, we coasted along within sight of the shores of Brazil. They are hilly and very woody, the green of the sloping banks being often interrupted by bright white patches, which seem to be of sand.

In the evening of Tuesday the 16th, we anchored in the bay of All Saints, opposite to the town of St Salvador, commonly called Bahia. It was quite dark before we got in, so that we lost the first entrance-view of that magnificent harbour, but the scattered lights show us the great extent and high situation of the town.

Wednesday, 17th

Early in the day we moved our anchorage closer in-shore, and then, on the invitation of Mr Pennell, the British consul, we went ashore to spend the day with him.

We landed at the arsenal, or rather dock-yard, where there is nothing of the neatness observable in such establishments at home. The first object we saw, however, was a fine 58-gun frigate on the stocks, the model of which I hear connoisseurs praise as beautiful. There is nothing besides the new ship, and some handsome pieces of old brass cannon, worth looking at. Every thing is visibly either suspended or on the decline, and there will probably be no improvement, until the political state of Brazil is a little more settled. We find things here, though not quite so unquiet as at Pernambuco, yet tending the same way.

The street into which we proceeded through the arsenal gate, forms, at this place, the breadth of the whole lower town of Bahia, and is, without any exception, the filthiest place I ever was in.

It is extremely narrow, yet all the working artificers bring their benches, and tools into the street. In the interstices between them, along the walls, are fruit-sellers, venders of sausages, black-puddings, fried fish, oil and sugar cakes, negroes plaiting hats or mats, caderas, (a kind of sedan chair,) with their bearers, dogs, pigs, and poultry, without partition or distinction. And as the gutter runs in the middle of the street, every thing is thrown there from the different stalls, as well as from the windows; and there the animals live and feed!

In this street are the warehouses and counting-houses of the merchants, both native and foreign. The buildings are high, but neither so handsome nor so airy as those of Pernambuco. . . .

We saw but little of the upper city, but that little was handsome, in our way to the consul's. His house, like those of all the British merchants, is a little way out of town, and is in the suburb Vittoria, . . .

Mr Pennell has most kindly given our young men a general invitation to his house, and accordingly, to-day several of them dined with him, and we had a party in the evening, when some of the ladies played quadrilles, while others danced.

Friday, 19th

I accompanied Miss Pennell in a tour of visits to her Portuguese friends. As it is not their custom to visit or be visited in the forenoon, it was hardly fair to take a stranger to see them. However, my curiosity, at least, was gratified.

In the first place, the houses, for the most part, are disgustingly dirty. The lower story usually consists of cells for the slaves, stabling &c. The staircases are narrow and dark, and, at more than one house, we waited in a passage while the servants ran to open the doors and windows of the sitting-rooms, and to call their mistresses, who were enjoying their undress in their own apartments.

When they appeared, I could scarcely believe that one half were gentlewomen. As they wear neither stay nor bodice, the figure becomes almost indecently slovenly, after very early youth, and this is the more disgusting, as they are very thinly clad, wearing no neck-handkerchiefs, and scarcely any sleeves.

Then, in this hot climate, it is unpleasant to see dark cottons and stuffs, without any white linen, near the skin. Hair black, ill combed, and dishevelled, or knotted unbecomingly, or still worse, en papillote,* and the whole person having an unwashed appearance.

When at any of the houses the bustle of opening the cobwebbed windows, and assembling the family was over, in two or three instances, the servants had to remove dishes of sugar, mandioc, and other provisions, which had been left in the best rooms to dry.

* In curl-papers!

There is usually a sofa at each end of the room, and to the right and left a long file of chairs, which look as if they never could be moved out of their place. Between the two sets of seats is a space, which, I am told, is often used for dancing, and in every house, I saw either a guitar or piano, and generally both.

Prints and pictures, the latter the worst daubs I ever saw, decorate the walls pretty generally, and there are, besides, crucifixes and other things of the kind.

Some houses, however, are more neatly arranged. One, I think belonging to a captain of the navy, was papered, the floors laid with mat, and the tables ornamented with pretty porcelain, Indian and French, the lady too was neatly dressed in a French wrapper. . . .

We were every where invited, after sitting a few moments on the sofa, to go to the balconies of the windows and enjoy the view and the breeze, or at least amuse ourselves with what was passing in the street.

And yet they did not lack conversation. The principal topic, however, was praise of the beauty of Bahia. Dress, children, and diseases, I think, made up the rest, and, to say the truth, their manner of talking on the latter subject is as disgusting as their dress, that is, in a morning. I am told they are different after dinner.

They marry very early, and soon lose their bloom. I did not see one tolerably pretty woman to-day. But then who is there that can bear so total a disguise as filth and untidiness spread over a woman?

Saturday, 20th

As the charts of this coast hitherto published are very incorrect, the captain asked permission from government to sound and survey the bay. It is refused on the ground of policy. As if it could be policy to keep hidden rocks and shoals, for one's own as well as other people's ships.

I walked through the greater part of the town. The lower part extends much farther than I could see the day I landed. It contains a few churches, one of which, belonging to a monastery of *A concepçaô*, is very handsome, but the smell within is disgusting. The flooring is laid in squares with stone, and within each square there is a panelling of wood about nine feet by six. Under each panel is a vault, into which the dead are thrown naked, until they reach a certain number, when with a little quicklime thrown in, the wood is fastened down, and then another square is opened, and so on in rotation.

From that church, passing the arsenal gate, we went along the low street, and found it widen considerably at three quarters of a mile beyond. There are the markets, which seem to be admirably supplied, especially with fish. There also is the slave market, a sight I have not yet learned to see without shame and indignation. Beyond are a set of arcades, where goldsmiths, jewellers, and haberdashers display their small wares, and there are the best-looking shops; but there is a want of neatness, of that art of making things look well, that invites a buyer in England and France. One bookseller's shop, where books are extravagantly dear, exists in the low town, and one other in the ascent to the upper. . . .

We ended our perambulation of the town, by going to the opera at night.

The theatre is placed on the highest part of the city, and the platform before it commands the finest view imaginable. It is a handsome building, and very commodious, both to spectators and actors. Within it is very large and well laid out, but dirty and in great want of fresh painting.

The actors are very bad as such, and little better as singers, but the orchestra is very tolerable. The piece was a very ill-acted tragedy, founded on Voltaire's *Mahomed*.

During the representation, the Portuguese ladies and gentlemen seemed determined to forget the stage altogether, and to laugh, eat sweetmeats, and drink coffee, as if at home. When the musicians, however, began to play the overture to the ballet, every eye and voice was directed to the stage, and a loud call for the national hymn followed, and not till it had been played again and again, was the ballet suffered to proceed.

During the bustle occasioned by this, a captain in the army was arrested and hurried out of the pit. Some say for picking pockets, others for using intemperate language on politics, when the national hymn was called for.

Meantime one of the midshipmen of our party had his sword stolen, adroitly enough, from the corner of the box, yet we perceived nobody enter, so that we conclude a gentleman in regimentals in the next box thought it would suit him, and so buckled it on to go home with. . . .

Monday 22d

This evening there was a large party, both Portuguese and English, at the consul's. In the well-dressed women I saw to-night, I had great difficulty in recognizing the slatterns of the other morning. The señhoras were all dressed after the French fashion, corset, fichu, garniture, all was proper, and even elegant, and there was a great display of jewels.

Our English ladies, though quite of the second rate of even colonial gentility, however, bore away the prize of beauty and grace. For after all, the clothes, however elegant, that are not worn habitually, can only embarrass and cramp the native movements, and, as Mademoiselle Clairon remarks, 'she who would *act* a gentlewoman in public, must *be* one in private life'.

The Portuguese men have all a mean look. None appear to have any education beyond counting-house forms, and their whole time is, I believe, spent between trade and gambling. In the latter, the ladies partake largely after they are married. Before that happy period, when there is no evening dance, they surround the card tables, and with eager eyes follow the game, and long for the time when they too may mingle in it.

I scarcely wonder at this propensity. Without education, and consequently without the resources of mind, and in a climate where exercise out of doors is all but impossible, a stimulus must be had, and gambling, from the sage to the savage, has always been resorted to, to quicken the current of life.

On the present occasion, we feared the young people would have been disappointed of their dance, because the fiddlers, after waiting some time, went away, as they alleged, because they had not their tea early enough. However, some of the ladies volunteered to play the piano, and the ball lasted till past midnight. . . .

Wednesday, October 24th

Mr Pennell, his daughter, and a few other friends joined us in an expedition to Itaparica, a large island that forms the western side of the Bay of All Saints. . . . Here it is not uncommon to give a slave his freedom, when he is too old or too infirm to work, that is, to turn him out of doors to beg or starve.

A few days ago, as a party of gentlemen were returning from a *picnic*, they found a poor negro woman lying in a dying state, by the side of the road. The English gentlemen applied to their Portuguese companions to speak to her, and comfort her, as thinking she would understand them better. But they said, 'Oh, 'tis only a black: let us ride on,' and so they did without further notice.

The poor creature, who was a dismissed slave, was carried to the English hospital, where she died in two days. Her diseases were age and hunger.

The slaves I saw here working in the distillery, appear thin, and I should say over-worked. But, I am told, that it is only in the distilling months that they appear so, and that at other seasons they are as fat and cheerful as those in the city, which is saying a great deal. They have a little church and burying-ground here, and as they see their little lot the lot of all, are more contented than I thought a slave could be. . . .

26th, 27th, 28th passed in pleasant enough intercourse with our countrymen . . . There are eighteen English mercantile houses established at Bahia, two French, and two German.

The English trade is principally carried on with Liverpool, which supplies manufactured goods and salt, in exchange for sugars, rums, tobaccos, cottons, very little coffee, and molasses. Lately, sugars have been shipped, on English account, for Hamburgh to a great extent, and I believe part of the returns are in German or Prussian woollen-cloths. The province of Bahia, by its neglect of manufactures, is quite dependent on commerce . . . but the chief trade of this place is *slaving*. This year no less than seventy-six slave-ships have sailed, without reckoning the smugglers in that line.

Sunday 28th

Mr Pennell had kindly fixed to-day for giving us a party in the country, and accordingly some of our young people were to go and assist in putting up tents, &c. But a miscalculation of tide and time, and a mistake as to the practicability of landing on part of the beach beyond the light-house, occasioned a variety of adventures and accidents, without which I have always heard no fête champêtre could be perfect.

However that may be, our party was a pleasant one. Instead of the tents, we made use of a country-house called the Roca, where beauty of situation, and neatness in itself and garden, made up for whatever we might have thought romantic in the tents, had they been erected.

It is the fashion to pave the courts of the country-houses here with dark pebbles, and to form in the pavement a sort of mosaic with milk-white shells. The gardens are laid out in alleys, something in the oriental taste. The millions of ants, which often in the course of a single night leave the best-clothed orange-tree bare both of leaves and flowers, render it necessary to surround each tree with a little stucco wall, or rather canal, in which there is water, till they are strong enough to recover if attacked by the ants. In the garden at Roca, every shrub of value, either for fruit or beauty, was so fenced, and there were seats, and water channels, and porcelain flower-pots, that made me almost think myself in the East.

But there is a newness in everything here, a want of interest on account of what has been, that is most sensibly felt. At most, we can only go back to the naked savage who devoured his prisoner, and adorned himself with bones and feathers here. In the East, imagination is at liberty to expatiate on past grandeur, wisdom, and politeness. Monuments of art and of science meet us at every step, *here*, every thing, nature herself, wears an air of newness, and the Europeans, so evidently foreign to the climate, and their African slaves, repugnant to every wholesome feeling, show too plainly that they are intruders, ever to be in harmony with the scene.

However, Roca is beautiful, and all those grave thoughts did not prevent us from delighting in the fair prospect of
'Hill and valley, fountain and fresh shade;'
nor enjoying the scent of oleander, jasmine, tuberose, and rose, although they are adopted, not native children of the soil.

Of the Portuguese society here I know so very little, that it would be presumptuous to give an opinion of it. I have met with two or three well-informed men of the world, and some lively conversable women, but none of either sex that at all reminded me of the well-educated men and women of Europe. . . .

Of those who read on political subjects, most are disciples of Voltaire, and they outgo his doctrines on politics, and equal his indecency as to religion, hence to sober people who have seen through the European revolutions, their discourses are sometimes disgusting. . . .

The English society is just such as one may expect. A few merchants, not of the first order, whose thoughts are engrossed by sugars and cottons, to the utter exclusion of all public matters that do not bear directly on their private trade, and of all matters of general science or information.

Not one knew the name of the plants around his own door. Not one is acquainted with the country ten miles beyond St Salvador's. Not one could tell me even the situation of the fine red clay, of which the only manufacture, pottery, here is made. In short, I was

41

completely out of patience with these incurious money-makers. . . .

The English are, however, hospitable and sociable among each other. They often dine together, the ladies love music and dancing, and some of the men gamble as much as the Portuguese.

Upon the whole, society is at a low, very low scale here among the English. Good eating and good drinking they contrive to have, for the flesh, fish, and fowl are good, fruits and vegetables various and excellent, and bread of the finest. Their slaves (for the English are all served by slaves), indeed, eat a sort of porridge of mandioc meal with small squares of jerked beef stirred into it, or, as their greatest luxury, stewed caravansas,* and this is likewise the principal food of the lower classes even of the free inhabitants. . . .

Friday, 2d November

Several of our people having yielded to the temptations of some worthless persons in the town, who induce sailors to desert in order that they themselves may profit by the premium given for the discovery of deserters, and having consequently swam on shore, the frigate has been moved up the harbour as far as Bom Fim, and it is intended to take her up still higher. . . .

Saturday, 3d November

Our plan of proceeding farther up the harbour is suspended for the present. The disputes between the European Portuguese and the Brazilians in the city, seem to be about to come to a crisis. Early this morning, we learned that troops were assembling from all quarters, and that therefore it was advisable, for the protection of the British property and the persons of the merchants, that the ship should return to her station opposite to the town.

The first provisional junta has lost several of its members, two of them being gone as delegates to Lisbon, and others being absent on account of ill health or disgust. The party opposing this junta talk loudly of independence, and wish at least one-half of the members of the provisional government to be native Brazilians. They also complain bitterly, that instead of redressing the evils they before endured, the junta has increased them by several arbitrary acts, and assert that one of the members who has a great grazing estate, has procured a monopoly, by which no man can

* Chick peas.

supply the market with beef without his permission, so that the city is ill supplied.

Such a ground of complaint will always excite popular indignation, and it appears now to be at its height. There has already been some skirmishing, in which, however, I hear there have been only three men killed.

The Brazilian artillery occupies Fort San Pedro, the governor, and the wreck of the junta, have the town and the palace. The governor, indeed, has arrested several, I think seventeen persons, in an arbitrary manner; among these, two of my acquaintance, Colonel Salvador and Mr Soares, and have put them, some on board the *Don Pedro*, some on board transports in the bay, for the purpose of transporting them to Lisbon. Some of these persons are not permitted to have any communication with their families, others, more favoured, are allowed to carry them with them. These are not the means to conciliate.

We have sent on shore to offer shelter to the ladies, and Captain Graham has agreed upon certain signals with the consul, in case of increased danger to his family.

Sunday, November 4th

On looking out at daylight this morning, we saw artillery planted, and troops drawn up on the platform opposite to the opera house.

I went on shore to see if Miss Pennell, her sister, or any of our other friends would come on board, but they naturally prefer staying to the last with their fathers and husbands.

Notwithstanding the warlike movements of these last two days, it appears most likely that the chiefs of the opposite parties will agree to await the decision of the Cortes* at Lisbon, with respect to their grievances, and at least a temporary peace will succeed to this disturbance.

It appears, however, next to impossible that things should remain as they are. The extreme inconvenience of having the supreme courts of justice so far distant as Lisbon must be more and more felt as the country increases in population and riches. The deputies to the Cortes are too far removed from their constituents to be guided in their deliberations or votes by them, and the establishment of so many juntas of government, each only accountable to the Cortes, must be a cause of internal disorder, if not of civil war, at no distant time.

* Portuguese parliament.

Monday 5th

A day of heavy tropical rain, which has forced both parties on shore to house their guns, and to desist for the present from all farther hostility. The governor, however, continues his arbitrary arrestations. It is curious how ancient authority awes men, for surely it is the accustomed obedience to the name of the king, and the dread of the name of rebellion, that prevents the Brazilians, armed as they are, from resisting these things.

Tuesday, November 6th

The *Morgiana*, Captain Finlaison, came in from Rio de Janeiro. She belongs to the African station, and came to Brazil about some prize business connected with the slave trade.

Captain Finlaison tells me tales that make my blood run cold, of horrors committed in the French slave-ships especially. Of young negresses, headed up in casks and thrown overboard, when the ships are chased. Of others, stowed in boxes when a ship was searched, with a bare chance of surviving their confinement. But where the trade is once admitted, no wonder the heart becomes callous to the individual sufferings of the slaves. The other day I took up some old Bahia newspapers, numbers of the *Idade d'Ouro*, and I find in the list of ships entered during three months of this year,

			Alive	Dead
1 slave ship from Moyanbique, 25th March, with			313	180
1 do.	–	6th March	378	61
1 do.	–	30th May	293	10
1 do.	–	29th June from Molendo,	357	102
1 do.	–	26th June	233	21
			1574	374

So that of the cargoes of these five ships reckoned thus accidentally, more than one in five had died on the passage!

It seems the English ships of war on the African coast are allowed to hire free blacks to make up their complements when deficient. There are several now on-board the *Morgiana*, two of whom are petty officers, and they are found most useful hands. They are paid and victualled like our own seamen.*

* The negroes of the *Cru* nation come to Sierra Leone from a great distance, and hire themselves out for any kind of labour, for six, eight, or ten months, sometimes for a year or two. They have then earned enough to go home and live like idle gentlemen, for at least twice that time, and then return to work. When their engagements on board men of war are fulfilled, they receive regular discharges and certificates.

Thursday, November 8

We went on board *Morgiana* to call on Mrs Macgregor, a lively intelligent Spaniard, who with her husband, Colonel Macgregor, is a passenger. She joined me in visits on shore, where the only news is, that the governor continues to arrest all persons suspected of favouring independence.

November 9

The Brazilians who occupy the forts of San Pedro and Santa Maria, had threatened to fire on the *Don Pedro*, if she attempted to get under weigh with the state prisoners on board. Nevertheless during the night she bent her sails, and sailed early this morning, carrying, it is said, twenty-eight gentlemen, who have been taken up without any ostensible reason. They are understood to have spoken in favour of the independence of Brazil.

Several of our officers went on shore to dine with the gentlemen of the English club, who meet once a month, to eat a very good dinner, and drink an immoderate quantity of wine for the honour of their country. . . .

16th

Several of our young people and I myself have begun to feel the bad effects of exposing ourselves too much to the sun and the rain. Yesterday I was so unwell as to put on a blister* for cough and pain in my side, and several of the others have slight degrees of fever. But generally speaking, the ship's company has been remarkably healthy.

Friday, 16th [sic]

Captain Graham taken suddenly and alarmingly ill. Towards evening he became better, and was able to attend to a most painful business.

Last night a man belonging to the *Morgiana* was killed, and the corporal of marines belonging to the ship severely wounded, on shore. It appears that neither of these men had so much as seen the murderer before. He had been drinking in the inner room of a venda with some sailors, and having quarrelled with one of them,

---

* A plaster which was supposed to draw out the poisons.

he fancied the rest were going to seize him, when he drew his knife to intimidate them, and rushed furiously out of the room.

The young man who was killed was standing at the outer door, waiting for one of his companions who was within, and the murderer seeing him there, imagined he also wished to stop him, and therefore stabbed him to the heart. Our corporal, who was passing by, saw the deed, and of course attempted to seize him, and in the attempt received a severe wound.

It is said, I know not with what truth, that Captain Finlaison is so hated here, on account of his activity against the slave trade, that none of his people are safe, and the death of the unfortunate man is attributed to that cause; but it appears to have been the result of a drunken quarrel. . . .

22d

At length all the invalids, excepting myself, are better. But, with another blister on, I can do little but write, or look from the cabin windows, and when I do look, I am sure to see something disagreeable.

This very moment, there is a slave-ship discharging her cargo, and the slaves are singing as they go ashore. They have left the ship, and they see they will be on the dry land, and so, at the command of their keeper, they are singing one of their country songs, in a strange land.

Poor wretches! could they foresee the slave-market, and the separation of friends and relations that will take place there, and the march up the country, and the labour of the mines, and the sugar-works, their singing would be a wailing cry.

But that 'blindness to the future kindly given', allows them a few hours of sad enjoyment.

This is the principal slave port in Brazil, and the negroes appear to me to be of a finer, stronger race, than any I have ever seen. One of the provisional junta of government is the greatest slave merchant here. Yet, I am happy to say, the Bahia press has lately actually printed a pamphlet against the slave trade.

Within the last year, seventy-six ships have sailed from this port for the coast of Africa, and it is well known that many of them will slave to the northward of the line, in spite of all treaties to the contrary. But the system of false papers is so cunningly and generally carried on, that detection is far from easy, and the difficulties that lie in the way of condemning any slave ship, render it a matter of hazard to detain them. An owner, however, is well satisfied, if one cargo in three arrives safe; and eight or nine successful voyages make a fortune.

Many Brazilian Portuguese have no occupation whatever. They lay out a sum of money in slaves, which slaves are ordered out every day, and must bring in a certain sum each night. These are the boatmen, chairmen, porters, and weavers of mats and hats that are to be hired in the streets and markets, and who thus support their masters.

24th

Yesterday the *Morgiana* sailed for Pernambuco, whence she will return to the coast of Africa. To-day the *Antigone* French frigate, commanded by Captain Villeneuve, nephew to the admiral of that name who was at Trafalgar, came in.

Whenever France and England are not at war, the French and English certainly seek each other, and like each other more than any other two nations. And yet they seem like two great heads of parties, and the other nations take the French and English sides, as if there were no cause of opposition but theirs.

Others may account for the fact, I am satisfied that it is so, and that whenever we meet a Frenchman in time of peace, in a distant country, it is something akin to the pleasure of seeing a country-man, and it is particularly the case with French naval men. Frequent intercourse of any kind, even that of war, begets a similarity of habits, manners, and ideas; so I suppose we have grown alike by fighting, and are all the more likely to fight again.

There is a report, but I believe not well founded, that placards are stuck up about the city threatening that all Europeans, especially Portuguese, who do not leave the place before the 24th of December, shall be massacred. I listen to these things, because reports, even when false, indicate something of the spirit of the times.

December 8th

This place is now so quiet that the merchants feel quite safe, and therefore we are leaving Bahia. I have taken leave of many hospitable persons who have shown us much attention, but my health is so indifferent, that but for the sake of that civility which I felt due to them, I should not have gone ashore again. However, it is all done, and we are in the act of getting under weigh. . . .

9 December 1821 – 10 January 1822

9th

As we sailed out of the bay, we amused ourselves with conjecturing the possible situation of Robinson Crusoe's plantation in the bay of All Saints. Those who had been at Cachoeira chose that it should be in that direction, while such as had been confined to the neighbourhood of the city pitched on different sitios, all or any of which might have answered the purpose.

There is a charm in Defoe's works that one hardly finds, excepting in the *Pilgrim's Progress*. The language is so homely, that one is not aware of the poetical cast of the thoughts, and both together form such a reality, that the parable and the romance alike remain fixed on the mind like truth. . . .

But we are once more upon the ocean, and our young people are again observing the stars, and measuring the distances of the planets. I grieve that one of the most promising of them is now an inmate in my cabin, in a very delicate state of health.* . . .

Rio de Janeiro, Saturday, December 15th, 1821

Nothing that I have ever seen is comparable in beauty to this bay. Naples, the Firth of Forth, Bombay harbour, and Trincomalee, each of which I thought perfect in their beauty, all must yield to this, which surpasses each in its different way.

Lofty mountains, rocks of clustered columns, luxuriant wood, bright flowery islands, green banks, all mixed with white buildings; each little eminence crowned with its church or fort; ships at anchor or in motion; and innumerable boats flitting about in such a delicious climate, – combine to render Rio de Janeiro the most enchanting scene that imagination can conceive. . . .

Monday, 17th

By the assistance of some friends ashore, we have procured a comfortable house in one of the suburbs of Rio, called the Catete, from the name of a little river which runs through it into the sea. To

---

* Midshipman Langford.

this house I have brought my poor suffering midshipman, Langford, and trust that free air, moderate exercise, and a milk diet, will restore him. We have been visited by several persons, who all appear hospitable and kind, particularly the acting consul-general, Col Cunningham, and his lady.

December 18th

I have begun house-keeping on shore. We find vegetables and poultry very good, but not cheap. Fruit is very good and cheap, butcher's meat cheap, but very bad. There is a monopolist butcher, and no person may even kill an animal for his own use without permission paid for from that person, consequently, as there is no competition, he supplies the market as he pleases.

The beef is so bad, that it can hardly be used even for soup meat, three days out of four, and that supplied to the ships is at least as bad. Mutton is scarce and bad, pork very good and fine. It is fed principally on mandioc and maize, near the town, that from a distance has the advantage of sugar cane.

Fish is not so plentiful as it ought to be, considering the abundance that there is on the whole coast, but it is extremely good, oysters, prawns, and crabs are as good as in any part of the world. . . .

We have hired a horse for our invalid, and I have borrowed one for myself. These animals are rather pretty at Rio, but far from strong; they are fed on maize and capim, or Guinea grass, which was introduced of late years into Brazil, and thrives pro-digiously. . . . The quantity necessary for each horse per day costs about eightpence, and his maize as much more. The common horses here sell for from twenty to one hundred dollars, the fine Buenos Ayres horses fetch a much higher price. Mules are generally used for carriages, being much hardier, and more capable of bearing the summer heat.

December 19th

I walked by the side of Langford's horse up one of the little valleys at the foot of the Corcorado. It is called the Laranjeiros, from the numerous orange trees which grow on each side of the little stream that beautifies and fertilizes it.

Just at the entrance to that valley, a little green plain stretches itself on either hand, through which the rivulet runs over its stony bed, and affords a tempting spot to groups of washerwomen of all hues, though the greater number are black, and they add not a little to the picturesque effect of the scene. They generally wear a red or white handkerchief round the head, and a full-plaited mantle tied over one shoulder, and passed under the opposite arm, with a full petticoat, is a favourite dress. Some wrap a long cloth round them, like the Hindoos, and some wear an ugly European frock, with a most ungraceful sort of bib tied before them.

Round the washerwoman's plain, hedges of acacia and mimosa fence the gardens of plantains, oranges, and other fruits which surround every villa, and beyond these, the coffee plantations extend far up the mountain, whose picturesque head closes the scene. . . .

Friday, December 21st

Mr Hayne, one of the commissioners of the slave trade commission, and his sister, having proposed a party to see the botanic gardens, we set off soon after day-light and drove to their house on the bay of Boto Fogo, perhaps the most beautiful spot in the neighbourhood of Rio, rich as it is in natural beauty, and its beauty is increased by the numerous and pretty country houses which now surround it. These have all grown up since the arrival of the court from Lisbon. . . .

The stream that waters the garden flows through a lovely valley, where the royal powder-mills are situated, but being fearful of too much exertion for Langford we put off visiting them to another day, and returned to the garden gate to breakfast.

His Majesty John VI built a small house there, with three or four rooms, to accommodate the royal party, when they visited the gardens. Our breakfast was prepared in the veranda of that house, from whence we had a charming view of the lake, with the mountains and woods, – the ocean, with three little islands that lie off the lake, and in the foreground a small chapel and village, at the extremity of a little smooth green plain.

After waiting with our agreeable and well-informed friends till the sea-breeze set in, we returned part of the way along the lake, and then ascended to the parsonage of Nossa Señhora da Cabeca, where we were joined by several other persons who had come to dine there with us. The Padre Manoel Gomez received us very kindly, and our pic-nic was spread in the ample veranda of his parsonage. . . .

To judge by the materials of the feast, so blended were the productions of every climate that we could scarcely have pronounced in what part of the world we were, had not the profusion of ananas and plantains, compared with the small quantity of apples and peaches, reminded us of it. As is usual on such occasions, the oldest inhabitants of Brazil praised most what came from afar, while *we* all gave the preference to the productions of the country.

I was soon drawn away from the table by the beauty of the prospect, which I endeavoured to sketch. . . .

As every body was determined to be pleased, we all felt sorry when it was time to separate. . . . We walked down to the foot of the hill, and each took his or her several conveyance; Colonel and Mrs Cunningham their comfortable English chariot, Mr and Miss Hayne their pretty curricle, and I my Rio caleche or *sege*, – a commodious but ugly carriage, very heavy, but well enough adapted to the rough roads between the garden and the town.

The gentlemen all rode, and most of us carried home something. Fruit and flowers attracted some, Langford got a number of diamond beetles, and a magnificent butterfly, and I a most inadequate sketch of the scene from the Padre's house.

December 27th

Since the jaunt to the botanical gardens, some of our invalids have been gaining ground, others who were well have become invalids, and I have done nothing but ride about or talk with them, and look at the beautiful views of the neighbourhood, and get a little better acquainted with the inhabitants, of whom the most amusing, so far as I have yet seen, are certainly the negroes, who carry about the fruit and vegetables for sale.

The midshipmen have made friends with some of them. One of them has become quite a friend in the house, and after he has sold his master's fruit, earns a small gratuity for himself, by his tales, his dances, and his songs.

His tribe, it seems, was at war with a neighbouring king, and he went out to fight when quite a boy, was taken prisoner, and sold.

This is probably the story of many, but our friend tells it with action and emphasis, and shows his wounds, and dances his war dance, and shouts his wild song, till the savage slave becomes almost a sublime object.

I have been for an hour to-night at a very different scene, a ball given by Mr B. a respectable English merchant. The Portuguese and Brazilian ladies are decidedly superior in appearance to those of Bahia. They look of higher caste, perhaps the residence of the court for so many years has polished them.

I cannot say the men partake of the advantage, but I cannot yet speak Portuguese well enough to dare to pronounce what either men or women really are. As to the English, what can I say? They are very like all one sees at home, in their rank of life, and the ladies, very good persons doubtless, would require Miss Austen's pen to make them interesting. However, as they appear to make no pretensions to any thing but what they are, to me they are good-humoured, hospitable, and therefore pleasing.

Monday, 31st Dec. 1821

I went to town for the first time; our road lay through the suburb of the Catete for about half a mile. Some handsome houses are situated on either hand, and the spaces between are filled with shops, and small houses inhabited by the families of the shop-keepers in town. . . .

There is in the city an air of bustle and activity quite agreeable to our European eyes, yet the Portuguese all take their siesta after dinner.

The negroes, whether free blacks or slaves, look cheerful and happy at their labour. There is such a demand for them, that they find full employment, and of course good pay, and remind one here as little as possible of their sad condition, unless, indeed, one passes the street of the Vallongo, then the slave-trade comes in all its horrors before one's eyes. On either hand are magazines of new slaves, called here *peices*, and there the wretched creatures are subject to all the miseries of a new negro's life, scanty diet, brutal examination, and the lash.

Tuesday, January 1st, 1822

I went to pay a second visit to an illustrious exile, Count Hogendorp, one of the Emperor Napoleon's generals. My first had been accidental.

One morning last week, riding with two of our young midshipmen, we came to a pleasant-looking cottage, high on the side of the Corcovado, and at the door we saw a very striking figure, to whom I instantly apologized for intruding on his grounds, saying that we were strangers, and had come there accidentally. He instantly, with a manner that showed him to be no common person, welcomed us, asked our names, and on being told them, said he had heard of us, and, but for his infirmities, would have called on us. He insisted on our dismounting, as a shower was coming on, and taking shelter with him.

By this time I perceived it was Count Hogendorp, and asked him if I had guessed rightly. He answered, yes; and added a few words, signifying that his master's servants, even in exile, carried that with them which distinguished them from other men.

The Count is the wreck of a once handsome man. He has not lost his martial air, he is tall, but not too thin, his grey eyes sparkle with intelligence, and his pure and forcible language is still conveyed in a clear well-toned voice, though a little the worse for age.

He ushered us into a spacious veranda, where he passes most of the day, and which is furnished with sofas, chairs, and tables. He then ordered his servant to bring breakfast. We had coffee, milk, and fresh butter, all the produce of his own farm, and as we sat, we saw the showers passing by and under us across the valley, which leads the eye to the bay below. The General entered frankly into conversation, and during breakfast, and while the shower lasted, spoke almost incessantly of his imperial master. . . .

On the annexation of Holland to France, he entered the French service with the rank of full colonel. He was always a great favourite with Napoleon, to whom his honesty and dis-interestedness in money matters seem to have been valuable, in proportion as these qualities were scarce among his followers.

The Count's affection for him is excessive, I should have said unaccountable, had he not shown me a letter written to him by the Emperor's own hand, on the death of his child, in which, besides much general kindness, there is even a touch of tenderness I had not looked for.

During the disastrous expedition to Russia, Hogendorp was entrusted with the government of Poland, and kept his court at Wilna. His last public service was performed in the defence of Hamburgh, where he was lieutenant governor. He would fain have attended the Emperor into exile, but that not being allowed, he came hither, where, with the greatest economy, and I believe, some assistance from the Prince,* who has great respect for him, he lives chiefly on the produce of his little farm.

Most of these particulars I learnt from himself, while resting and sheltered from the rain, which lasted nearly an hour.

He then showed me his house, which is small indeed, consisting of only three rooms, besides the veranda; his study, where a few

* Don Pedro of Brazil.

books, two or three casts from antique bas reliefs, and some maps and prints, indicate the retirement of a gentleman; his bedroom, the walls of which, with a capricious taste, are painted black, and on that sombre ground, skeletons of the natural size, in every attitude of glee, remind one of Holbein's Dance of Death; and a third room occupied by barrels of orange wine, and jars of liqueur made of the grumaxama (at least as agreeable as cherry brandy which it resembles), the produce of his farm; and the sale of which, together with his coffee, helps out his slender income.

The General, as he loves to be called, led us round his garden, and displayed with even fondness, his fruits and his flowers, extolled the climate, and only blamed the people, for the neglect and want of industry, which wastes half the advantages God has given them.

On returning to the house, he introduced to me his old Prussian servant (who has seen many a campaign with him) and his negroes, whom he freed on purchasing them. He has induced the women to wear a nose jewel, after the fashion of Java, which he seems to remember with particular pleasure. I was sorry to leave the Count, but was afraid some alarm might be felt at home concerning us, and therefore bade him adieu. . . .

January 8th, 1822

To-day we left the house on shore, and are again at home on board the *Doris*, with all our invalids much better. . . .

Wednesday, January 9th

To-day is expected to be a day of much importance to the future fate of Brazil. But I must go back to the arrival of a message from the Cortes at Lisbon, intimating to the Prince their pleasure, that he should forthwith repair to Europe, and begin his education, and proceed to travel incognito through Spain, France, and England.

This message excited the most lively indignation not only in His Royal Highness, but in the Brazilians from one end of the Kingdom to the other. The Prince is willing to obey the orders of his father and the Cortes, at the same time he cannot but feel as a man the want of decency of the message, and being thus bid to go home, and especially forbidden to carry any guards with him, as it should seem, lest they might have contracted too much attachment for his person.

The Brazilians regard this step as preliminary to removing from this country the courts of justice, which have for fourteen years been held here, and so removing causes to Lisbon, by which means, Brazil would be again reduced to the condition of a dependent colony instead of enjoying equal rights and privileges with the mother country, a degradation they are by no means inclined to submit to.

10th

Yesterday there was a meeting of the camara* of Rio, and after a short consultation the members went in procession, accompanied by a great concourse of people, to the Prince, with a strong remonstrance against his leaving the country, and an earnest entreaty that he would remain among his faithful people.

His Royal Highness received them graciously, and replied, that since it appeared to be the wish of all, and for the good of all, he would remain. This declaration was received with shouts of enthusiasm, which were answered by the discharge of artillery, and every mark of public rejoicing. . . .

* The legislative chamber.

10 January – 20 April 1822

January 10th

To-day our friends the merchants are under fresh alarm, and have made a formal request to the captain to stay. With that petty spirit which passes for *diplomatic*, the deputy-consul and merchants, instead of saying what they are afraid of, only say, 'Sir, we are afraid, circumstances make us so, and we hope you will stay till,' &c. &c.; as much as to say, 'You are answerable for evil, if it happens,' although they are too much afraid of committing themselves to say why.

I do not trouble myself now about their official reports, which I perceive are large sheets of paper, and large seals, without one word that might not be published on every church wall, for their milk and water tenor, but which I consider as absurd and mischievous, because they tend to excite distrust and alarm where no danger is.

The truth is now, that there might be some cause of fear, if they would openly express it. The language of the Portuguese officers is most violent. They talk of carrying the Prince by main force to Lisbon, and so making him obey the Cortes in spite of the Brazilians, and both parties are so violent, that they will probably fight. In that fight there will doubtless be danger to foreign property; but why not say so? why not say such is the case? . . . .

11th

There is a great deal of uneasiness to-day. The Portuguese commander-in-chief of the troops, General Avilez, has demanded and received his discharge.

It is said, perhaps untruly, that his remonstrance to the Prince against his remaining here has been ungentlemanlike and indecent. I hear the troops will not consent to his removal, and they are particularly incensed that the choice of a successor should fall on General Curado, a Brazilian, who, it is said, will be called from St Paul's to succeed Avilez.

He is a veteran, who has commanded with distinction in all the campaigns on the southern frontier, and his actions are better known among his countrymen than those distant battles in Europe, on which the Portuguese officers of every rank are apt to pride themselves here, however slight the share they had in them, to the annoyance of the Brazilians.

12th

Yesterday the military commission for the government of the army here was broke up, and Curado appointed commander-in-chief, and minister of war.

The Portuguese General Avilez made his appearance at the barracks of the European soldiers to take leave of them. They were under arms to receive him, and vowed not to part with him, or to obey another commander, and were with difficulty reduced to such order as to promise tolerable tranquillity for the day at least.

It is said, that as it had been understood that they had expressed some jealousy, because the guard of honour at the opera-house had been for the two last evenings composed of Brazilians, the Prince sent to the Portuguese barracks for the guard of last night, but that they refused to go, saying, that as His Royal Highness was so partial to the Brazilians, he had better continue to be guarded by them. I am not sure this is true, but from the circumstances of the day it is not improbable.

The opera-house was again brilliantly lighted. The Prince and Princess were there, and had been received as well as on the ninth, when, at about eleven o'clock, the Prince was called out of his box, and informed that bodies of from twenty to thirty of the Portuguese soldiers were parading the streets, breaking windows and insulting passengers in their way from barrack to barrack, where everything wore the appearance of determined mutiny.

At the same time, a report of these circumstances having reached the house, the spectators began to rise for the purpose of going home. The Prince, having given such orders as were necessary, returned to the box, and going with the Princess (then near her confinement) to the front, he addressed the people. He assured them that there was nothing serious, that he had already given orders to send the riotous soldiers, who had been quarrelling with the blacks, back to their barracks, and entreated them not to leave the theatre and increase the tumult, by their presence in the street, but remain till the end of the piece, as he meant to do, when he had no doubt all would be quiet.

The coolness and presence of mind of the Prince, no doubt, preserved the city from much confusion and misery. By the time the opera was over the streets were sufficiently clear to permit every one to go home in safety.

Meantime the Portuguese troops, to the number of seven hundred, had marched up to the Castle-hill, commanding the principal streets in the town, and had taken with them four pieces of artillery, and threatened to sack the town.

The field-pieces belonging to the Brazilians, which had remained in the town after the 26th of February, had been sent to the usual station of the artillery, at the botanical gardens, no longer ago than last week, so they entertained no fear of artillery. But they were disappointed in their expectation of being joined by that part of the Portuguese force which was stationed at San Cristovao. This amounted to about five hundred men, who said the King had left them to attend on the person of the Prince, and they had nothing to do with anything else. A declaration that was looked on with suspicion by the Brazilians.

While the Portuguese were taking up their new and threatening position, the Brazilians were not idle. Every horse and mule in the town was pressed, and expresses despatched to all the militia regiments, and other Brazilian troops, as well as to the head-quarters of the artillery.

The Prince was most active, so that by four o'clock this morning (12th), he found himself at the head of a body of four thousand men, in the Campo de Santa Anna, not only ready, but eager for action; and though deficient in discipline, formidable from their numbers and determination. . . .

I went ashore with an officer as early as I could, chiefly for the purpose of seeing the troops in the Campo de Santa Anna. In consequence, however, of the press of horses and mules, it was some time before I could get a chaise to convey me there, and it was much too hot to walk.

At length, however, I procured one, and determined to call on the Viscondeca of Rio Seco in my way, to offer her refuge in the frigate. We found her in a Brazilian dishabille, and looking harassed and anxious. She had remained in the theatre as long as the Prince last night, and had then hurried home to provide for the safety of her family and her jewels. Her family she had despatched to her estate in the country. For the jewels, she had them all packed in small parcels, intending to escape with them herself in disguise to us, in case of a serious attack on the city, and she had left a quantity of valuable plate exposed in different parts of the house to occupy the soldiers on their first entrance.

Everything, however, looks better now, and we assured her we had seen the first part of one of the Lisbon regiments ready to embark* as we landed. We promised her, that on her making a signal from her house, or sending a message, she should have protection. She appears very apprehensive of evil from the liberation of the prisoners by the Brazilians during the night, and says, that there are some fears that the Portuguese will seize the forts on the other side, and hold them till the arrival of the reinforcements daily expected from Lisbon. This would indeed, be disastrous; but I believe the apprehension to be ill founded. . . .

On our return to the ship, we were stopped for some time in the palace square, by a great concourse of people assembled to witness the entrance of the first Brazilian guard into the palace, while the last Portuguese guard marched out, amid the loud huzzas of the people. And on reaching the stairs, where we were to embark, we found the last of one regiment, and the first of another, about to sail for the Praya Grande, so that the city may sleep in security to-night.

The inhabitants generally, but especially the foreign merchants, are well pleased to see the Lisbon troops dismissed, for they have long been most tyrannically brutal to strangers, to negroes, and not unfrequently to Brazilians. And, for many weeks past, their arrogance has been disgusting to both Prince and people.

The appearance of the city is melancholy enough, the shops are shut up, guards are parading the streets, and every body looks anxious. The shopkeepers are all employed as militia. They are walking about with bands and belts of raw hides over their ordinary clothes, but their arms and ammunition were all in good order, and excepting these and the English, I saw nobody at all out of doors.

13th

Every thing seems quiet to-day. From the ship we see the rest of the troops going over to the Praya Grande. Yet there is necessarily a great deal of anxiety among all classes of persons.

Some persons have sent some of their valuables on board the frigate, for safety, and a message, I do not know on what authority, arrived to know if the Prince and Princess, and family, could be received and protected on board.

The answer, of course, is, that though the ship must observe the

---

* The Prince had ordered them to embark for Portugal. They were to go to the Praya Grande until ships were available to take them to Lisbon.

strictest neutrality between the parties, yet that we are ready at once to receive and protect the Princess and children, and also, whenever he has reason to apprehend personal danger, the Prince himself. My cabin is therefore ready. I hope they will not be forced to come afloat. The more they can trust to the Brazilians the better for them, and for the cause of that independence which is now so inevitable, that the only question is whether it shall be obtained with or without bloodshed.

We have determined to have a ball on board, the day after to-morrow, that the people may get acquainted with us, – and then if any thing occurs to render it advisable to take refuge with us, they will know who they are to come amongst. . . .

15th

Our ball went off very well. We had more foreigners than English, and as there was excellent music from the opera-orchestra, and a great deal of dancing, the young people enjoyed it much. I should have done so also, but that Captain Graham was suffering with the gout so severely, that I could have wished to put off the dance.

I had commissioned the Viscondeca do Rio Seco and some other ladies to bring their Portuguese friends, which they did, and we had a number of pretty and agreeable women, and several gentlemanlike men, in addition to our English friends.

A dance on ship-board is always agreeable and picturesque. There is something in the very contrast afforded by the furniture of the deck of a ship of war to the company and occupation of a ball that is striking.

> The little warlike world within,
> The well-reeved guns and netted canopy,

all dressed with evergreens and flowers, waving over the heads of gay girls and their smiling partners, furnish forth combinations in which poetry and romance delight, and which one must be stoical indeed to contemplate without emotion. I never loved dancing myself, perhaps because I never excelled in it, but yet, a ball-room is to me a delightful place. . . .

17th

Nothing remarkable yesterday or to-day, but the perfect quiet of the town. The Prince goes on discharging the soldiers. . . .

20th

The *Aurora* arrived from Pernambuco and Bahia, at both which places it appears that every thing is quiet. But as the meeting of the camara of Bahia is to take place early next month, for the purpose of chusing a new provisional government, the English are apprehensive of some disturbance, and therefore we are to return thither to protect our friends in case of need.

21st

I went ashore to shop with Glennie. There are a good many English shops, such as saddlers, and stores, not unlike what we call in England an Italian warehouse, for eatables and drinkables, but the English here generally sell their goods wholesale to native or French retailers. The latter have a great many shops of mercery, haberdashery, and millinery. For tailors, I think, there are more English than French, and but few of either.

There are bakers' shops of both nations, and plenty of English pot-houses, whose *Union Jacks*, *Red Lions*, *Jolly Tars*, with their English inscriptions, vie with those of Greenwich or Deptford. The goldsmiths all live in one street, called by their name *Rua dos Ourives*, and their goods are exposed in hanging frames at each side of the shop-door or window, in the fashion of two centuries back. The workmanship of their chains, crosses, buttons, and other ornaments, is exquisite, and the price of the labour, charged over the weight of the metal, moderate.

Most of the streets are lined with English goods. At every door the words *London superfine* meet the eye. Printed cottons, broad cloths, crockery, but above all, hardware from Birmingham, are to be had little dearer than at home, in the Brazilian shops, besides silks, crapes, and other articles from China. But any thing bought by retail in an English or French shop is, usually speaking, very dear.

I am amused at the apparent apathy of the Brazilian shop-keepers. If they are engaged, as now is not unfrequently the case, in talking politics, or reading a newspaper, or perhaps only enjoying a cool seat in the back of their shop, they will often say they have not the article enquired for, rather than rise to fetch it. And if the customer persists and points it out in the shop, he is coolly desired to get it for himself, and lay down the money.

This happened several times during the course of our search for some tools for turning to-day along the Rua Direita, where every second house is a hardware shop, furnished from Sheffield and Birmingham.

22d

The Princess's birthday was celebrated by firing of cannon, a review, and a drawing-room. Capt. Prescott, of the *Aurora*, and Capt. Graham, attended it. It seems the Prince took little or no notice of them, or any of the English. I think it probable that the Brazilians are jealous of us, on account of our long alliance with Portugal, and besides, they may take the converse of the maxim, 'those that are not against us are for us': and think because we are not for them, we are against them.

Two days later the Doris *sailed for Bahia, where the forthcoming election of a provisional government favourable to independence threatened possible disturbance to the English merchants.*

In the event, though Maria discerned an enthusiastic republican spirit among the townsfolk, the English appeared unalarmed. The ship's company were entertained to three balls, and Maria had time to ride out and explore the surrounding country where she noted the oranges and mangoes ripening.

On their return to Rio, they found the Prince, Don Pedro, had dismissed the Portuguese troops, threatening that if they did not at once embark as ordered, he would 'give them such a breakfast of Brazilian balls as should make them glad to leave the country'.[1]

Friday, March 1st

The weather is now excessively hot, the thermometer being seldom under 88°, and we have had it on board at 92° Fahrenheit.

Capt. Graham has had a slight attack of gout, for which reason I have not been ashore since our return from Bahia; but as he is a little better to-day he has insisted on my accompanying a party of our young men in an expedition up the harbour to see a country estate and factory.

At one o'clock, our friend, Mr N— called for us, with a large boat of the country, which is better for the purpose than our ship's boats. . . .

The place we were going to is Nossa Señhora da Luz, about twelve miles from Rio, up the harbour, near the mouth of the river Guaxindiba, which river rises in the hills of Taypu; . . .

We found, that owing to our neglect in not sending beforehand to announce our visit, neither the master of the house nor his housekeeper were at home. However, Mr N— being an old friend, went into the poultry yard, and ordered thence an excellent supper, and while it was preparing, we went to look at the pottery, which is only for the coarsest red ware. . . . Leaving the pottery, we climbed the hill that marks the first approach to N. S. da Luz. . . .

The moon was up long before we returned from our ramble, and long before our host arrived. . . .

As we were looking over the bay, a larger boat appeared. It neared the shore, and our host, Mr Lewis P—, who superintends the fazenda, landed, and kindly received our apology for coming without previous notice. . . .

He led the way to the garden, where we passed the time till supper was ready. The midshipmen found more oranges, and better than they had yet met with, and did full justice to them. . . .

2d

I rose at daylight, and rode with Mr N— through the estate, while Mr Dance, my cousin Glennie, and the two boys, went to shoot in the marsh by the river side. . . .

I returned well pleased from my ride, and found my young sportsmen not less pleased with their morning's ramble.

Not, indeed, that they had shot snipes, as they intended, but they had gotten a huge lizard (*Lacerta Marmorata*), of a kind they had not seen before. They had seen the large land-crab (*Ruricola*), and they had brought down a boatswain bird, a sort of pelican (*Pelicanus Lencocephalus*), which they proposed to stuff. Accordingly after breakfast, as the weather was too hot to walk farther, the bird and the lizard were both skinned, the guns were cleaned, and I made a sketch of the landscape. . . .

Sunday, 3d

I went out before breakfast, with a negro carpenter for my guide. This man, with little instruction, has learned his art so as to be not only a good carpenter and joiner, but also a very tolerable cabinet-maker, and in other respects displays a quickness of understanding which gives no countenance to the pretended inferiority of negro intellect. I was much pleased with the observations he made on many things which I remarked as new, and with the perfect understanding he seemed to have of all country works.

After breakfast, I attended the weekly muster of all the negroes of the fazenda. Clean shirts and trowsers were given the men, and shifts and skirts to the women, of very coarse white cotton. Each, as he or she came in, kissed a hand, and then bowed to Mr P— saying either 'Father, give me blessing', or 'The names of Jesus and Mary be praised!' and were answered accordingly, either 'Bless you', or 'Be they praised'.

This is the custom in old establishments. It is repeated morning and evening, and seems to acknowledge a kind of relationship between master and slave. It must diminish the evils of slavery to one, the tyranny of mastership in the other, to acknowledge thus a common superior Master on whom they both depend.

As each slave passed in review, some questions were asked concerning himself, his family, if he had one, or his work, and each received a portion of snuff or tobacco, according to his taste.

Mr P— is one of the few persons whom I have met conversant among slaves, who appears to have made them an object of rational and humane attention. He tells me that the creole negroes and mulattoes are far superior in industry to the Portuguese and Brazilians, who, from causes not difficult to be imagined, are far the most indolent and ignorant.

The negroes and mulattoes have strong motives to exertion of every kind, and succeed in what they undertake accordingly. They are the best artificers and artists. The orchestra of the opera-house is composed of at least one-third of mulattoes. All decorative painting, carving, and inlaying is done by them; in short, they excel in all ingenious mechanical arts. . . .

4th

I was very sorry indeed this morning at sunrise, when I saw the boats ready to convey us from N. S. da Luz, where we had enjoyed our three days as much as possible. . . . We returned to the ship by a different way from that by which we went, through the archipelago of beautiful islands on the eastern side of the harbour; and I had the pleasure to find the Captain really better, though still with tender feet. . . .

7th

The *Superb* arrived from Valparaiso, bringing no news of importance. Indeed, if she had, we are scarcely in a state to attend to it, we have sat up all night with B., one of our midshipmen, who is dangerously ill.

8th

Captain Graham not feeling well enough to leave the ship. I went with Captain Prescott of the *Aurora*, to visit the French Commodore Roussin on board the *Amazone*. I have seldom been better pleased. The captains of the other French ships were there, to receive us. All the urbanity of Frenchmen, joined with the delightful frankness of the profession, assured us we were welcome.

The ship itself, every part of which we saw, is a model of all that can be done, either in the dock-yard at home, or by officers afloat, for comfort, health, and cleanliness, and is well as a man of war. Her captain, however, is a superior man, and many ships of every and any nation might be visited before his equal would be met with.

I wish it were possible that we should introduce into our ships the oven on the lower deck, which gives fresh bread twice a week for the whole ship's company, not only for the sake of the bread, but the heating it must air and ventilate the ship.

9th

The Portuguese squadron from Lisbon, with a reinforcement of troops, arrived off the harbour. Troops are sent to reinforce the garrisons in the forts, at the entrance, and the ships are forbidden to enter, but promised victuals and water to carry them to Lisbon.

I was on shore all day on business, preparatory to our sailing for Valparaiso. Captain Graham being too unwell to venture out of the ship himself, he therefore undertook to nurse the invalid for me. I returned late. I found B. dangerously ill, and Captain Graham very uneasy.

I received many persons on board, and took leave of many.

10th

We sailed at daylight from Rio, in full hope that the cool weather we shall find on going round Cape Horn, and the fine climate of Chile, will do us all good.

I have not been in bed for three nights. My invalids are in that state, that night watching is necessary for them.

13th

In addition to our other troubles, the first lieutenant is taken dangerously ill. But Captain Graham appears better, though not yet able to go on deck.

16th

Yesterday afternoon the mercury in the barometer sunk in a very short space of time a whole inch, and we had a gale of wind. The cold is sensibly increased . . . and we have many sick. B. is getting better.

17th

Wind and sea abated, and the barometer rising once more. The mercury stands at thirty inches and two-tenths. I have lain down at four o'clock these two mornings, Glennie having kindly relieved my watching at that hour. We have removed the dead-lights* from the cabin windows.

18th

Every thing better. The young people again at school. . . .

On the *19th* and *20th* the mercury in the barometer sunk gradually from 30 to 29–02, and rose again as before on the 21st. It blew hard . . . There are many albatrosses and stormy petrels about the ship. . . .

24th

. . . Seeing two penguins to-day, we supposed some land must be near, but found no bottom with 100 fathoms line. The cold weather seems to have a good effect on our invalids. The barometer fell suddenly, and a strong S.W. wind succeeded, and we were glad to light a fire in the cabin. . . .

25th

. . . Strong south-westerly gales and heavy sea. . . . We are in the midst of a dark boisterous sea. Over us, a dense, grey, cold sky. The albatross, stormy petrel, and pintado are our companions, yet

* Storm shutters.

there is a pleasure in stemming the apparently irresistible waves, and in wrestling thus with the elements.

I forget what writer it is who observes, that the sublime and the ridiculous border on each other. I am sure they approach very nearly at sea.

If I look abroad, I see the grandest and most sublime object in nature, – the ocean raging in its might, and man, in all his honour, and dignity, and powers of mind and body, wrestling with and commanding it. Then I look within, round my little home in the cabin, and every roll of the ship causes accidents irresistibly ludicrous, and in spite of the inconveniences they bring with them, one cannot choose but laugh.

Sometimes, in spite of all usual precautions, of cushions and clothes, the breakfast-table is suddenly stripped of half its load, which is lodged in the lee scuppers, whither the coal-scuttle and its contents had adjourned the instant before. Then succeed the school-room distresses of *capsized* ink-stands, broken slates, torn books, and lost places. Not to mention the loss of many a painful calculation, and other evils exquisite in their kind, but abundantly laughable, especially, as it happened just now, if the schoolmaster is induced to measure his length on the deck, when in the act of reprimanding the carelessness which subjects the slates and books to these untoward chances.

28th

. . . Captain Graham and the first lieutenant still both very ill.

At one o'clock this morning the mercury in the barometer sunk to 28–09. At seven it rose again to 29–01.

The thermometer is at 38° of Fahrenheit, and we have had squalls of snow and sleet, and a heavy sea. There are flocks of very small birds about the ship, and we have seen a great many whales.

30th

. . . A violent gale of wind from the south-west, the only thing like a hard gale since we left England.

I had breakfast spread on the cabin desk, as it was not possible to secure any thing on a table. Clarke, one of the quarter-masters, had two ribs broken by a fall on deck, and Sinclair, a very strong man, was taken ill after being an hour at the wheel.

We have made gloves for the men at the wheel of canvass, lined with dreadnought,* and for the people at night, waistbands of canvass, with dreadnought linings.

The snow and hail squalls are very severe, ice forms in every fold of the sails. This is hard upon the men, so soon after leaving Rio in the hottest part of the year. . . .

April 1st

. . . the weather much more mild and moderate. Our young men have caught a number of birds, principally petrels, the *P. Pelagica*, or Mother Cary's chicken, is the least, the *P. Pintado* is gayest on the water. But the *P. Glacialis*, or fulmer, is most beautiful when brought on board, I cannot enough admire the delicate beauty of the snow-white plumage, unwet and unsoiled, amid the salt waves. The poets have scandalized both the arctic and antarctic regions as

> A bleak expanse,
> Shagg'd o'er with wavy rocks, cheerless and *void*
> Of ev'ry life;

yet, on Capt. Parry's† approach to the north pole, he found the solitude teeming with *life*, and the farther south we have sailed, the more *life* we have found on the waters.

Yesterday the sea was covered with albatrosses, and four kinds of petrel. The penguin comes near us, shoals of porpoises are constantly flitting by, and whales for ever rising to the surface and blowing alongside of the ship.

With the thermometer not lower than 30°, we feel the cold excessive. Yesterday morning the main rigging was cased in ice, and the ropes were so frozen after the sleet in the night, that it was difficult to work them. . . .

I was glad to-day, when the dead-lights were removed, to see the bright, blue, but still boisterous sea, spreading with ample waves curled with snowy tops, in the sunshine. It is many days since we have seen the sun, and the white birds flying and chattering, or wrestling on the water, while the ship, like them, sometimes bravely mounts the very top of the wave, and sometimes quietly subsides with it. . . .

* A thick cloth.
† Sir William Edward Parry (1790–1855), English rear-admiral and Arctic explorer. In 1820 he had got half-way to solving the mystery of a North West passage.

April 2d

A few minutes after noon, an iceberg was reported on the lee-bow. As I had never seen one, I went on deck for the first time since we left Rio to see it.

It appeared like a moderately high conical hill, and looked very white upon the bleak grey sky. It might be about twelve miles from us. . . .

For some few days the violent motion of the ship, occasioned by the heavy sea, has rendered writing and drawing irksome, for, as Lord Dorset's song has it,

> Our paper, pens, and ink, and we,
> Roll up and down our ships, at sea.

Nevertheless we are not idle. As the cabin has always a good fire in it, it is the general rendezvous for invalids, and the midshipmen come in and out as they please, as it is the school-room.

In one corner Glennie has his apparatus for skinning and dissecting the birds we take, and we have constantly occasion to admire the beautiful contrivances of nature in providing for her creatures.

These huge sea-birds, that we find so far from any land, have on each side large air-vessels adapted for floating them in the air, or on the water, they are placed below the wings, and the liver, gizzard and entrails rest on them. In each gizzard of those we have yet opened, there have been two small pebbles, of unequal size, and the gizzard is very rough within. We have found more vegetable than animal food in their stomachs. . . .

Next morning Captain Graham became critically ill. But although she steadfastly kept her journal between now and her husband's death six days later, Maria could not bring herself to copy out that 'register of acute suffering'[2] when she came to edit her work for publication two years later, only recording that 'On the night of the ninth of April, I regularly undressed and went to bed for the first time since I left Rio de Janeiro. All was then over, and I slept long and rested. . . .'[3]

Throughout her ordeal she had been kept going by the kindness of the ship's surgeons, and particularly by the affectionate behaviour of 'my boys', as the midshipmen were called. And when it was ended, she had the wan comfort that at least no stranger's hand had closed her husband's eyes, nor smoothed his pillow. But the experience left her totally alone, and a widow, and, as she expressed it, 'with half the globe between me and my kindred . . .'.[4]

3

Chile Journal

28 April – 12 June 1822

When the Doris *anchored off Valparaiso in late April 1822, Chile had been independent from Spain for only four years.*

In 1817 the Argentinian-born patriot, Jose San Martin, had daringly led his small army through the high passes of the Andes into Chile to support the country's patriots who were fighting a losing war against the army of Spanish counter-revolutionaries.

The Spanish were defeated at Chacabuco, but when the Chileans offered San Martin the government of the country he declined in favour of the Chileno general, Bernardo O'Higgins. For San Martin's ultimate goal was no less than the defeat of Spanish opposition to South American independence, and this was centred in Peru.

O'Higgins called the first provisional government of the new republic at Santiago, and in two years succeeded in raising money and men to equip a Chileno navy under the British mercenary, Lord Cochrane,* and an army of liberation with San Martin as commander-in-chief to invade Peru.

The cost of this, however, had been an authoritarian and increasingly unpopular style of government, and by the time Maria arrived in Chile it was running into difficulties.

His Majesty's ship Doris, *Valparaiso harbour, Sunday night, April 28th, 1822.*

To-day the newness of the place, and all the other circumstances of our arrival, have drawn my thoughts to take some interest in the things around me. I can conceive nothing more glorious than the

---

* Thomas Cochrane, later 10th Earl of Dundonald (1775–1860).

sight of the Andes this morning on approaching the land at day-break. Starting, as it were, from the ocean itself, their summits of eternal snow shone in all the majesty of light long before the lower earth was illuminated. Suddenly the sun appeared from behind them and they were lost, and we sailed on for hours before we descried the land.

On anchoring here to-day, the first object I saw was the Chile State's brig *Galvarino*, formerly the British brig of war *Hecate*,* the first ship my husband ever commanded, and in which I sailed with him in the Eastern Indian seas. Twelve years have since passed away!

We found His Majesty's ship *Blossom* here. Her commander, Captain Vernon, will, I believe, take the command of this ship to-morrow.

The United States' ships *Franklin* and *Constellation* are also here. As soon as Commodore Stewart saw the *Doris* approach the harbour with her colours half-mast high, he came to offer every assistance and accommodation the ship might require, and hearing that I was on board he returned, bringing Mrs Stewart to call on me, and to offer me a cabin in the *Franklin*, in case I preferred it to remaining here, until I could procure a room on shore.

Monday, 29th

This has been a day of trial. Early in the morning the new captain's servants came on board to prepare the cabin for their master's reception. I believe, what must be done is better done at once.

Soon after breakfast, Captain Ridgely, of the United States' ship *Constellation*, brought Mrs and Miss Hogan, the wife and daughter of the American consul, to call and to offer all the assistance in their power, and told me, that the Commodore had delayed the sailing of his frigate, the *Constellation*, in order that she might carry letters from the *Doris* round Cape Horn, and would delay it still farther if I wished to avail myself of the opportunity to return home immediately.

I was grateful, but declined the offer. I feel that I have neither health nor spirits for such a voyage just yet.

Immediately afterwards, Don Jose Ignacio Zenteno, the governor of Valparaiso, with two other officers, came on board on a visit of humanity as well as respect. He told me that he had appointed a spot within the fortress where I may 'bury my dead

---

* She had been bought by two English officers, Captains Guise and Spry, and then brought to Chile on speculation where she was bought by the government.

out of my sight', with such ceremonies and honours as our church and service demand, and has promised the attendance of soldiers, &c. All this is kind, and it is liberal.

At four o'clock I received notice that Mrs Campbell, a Spanish lady, the wife of an English merchant, would receive me into her house until I could find a lodging, and I left the ship shortly afterwards.

I hardly know how I left it, or how I passed over the deck where one little year ago I had been welcomed with such different prospects and feelings.

I have now been two hours ashore. Mrs Campbell kindly allows me the liberty of being alone, which is kinder than any other kindness she could show.

April 30th

This afternoon I stood at my window, looking over the bay.

The captain's barge, of the *Doris*, brought ashore the remains of my indulgent friend, companion, and husband. There were all his own people, and those of the *Blossom* and of the American ships, and their flags joined and mingled with those of England and of Chile.

Their musicians played together the hymns fit for the burial of the pure in heart. The procession was long, and joined by many who thought of those far off, and perhaps now no more, and by many from respect to our country. I believe, indeed I know, that all was done that the pious feelings of our nature towards the departed demand, and if such things could soothe such a grief as mine they were not wanting. . . .

May 6th

I have been very unwell, meantime my friends have procured a small house for me at some distance from the port, and I am preparing to remove to it.

9th of May, 1822

I took possession of my cottage at Valparaiso, and felt indescribable relief in being quiet and alone. . . .

The Almendral is full of olive groves, and of almond gardens, whence it has its name; but, though far the pleasantest part of the town, it is not believed to be safe to live in it, lest one should be robbed or murdered, so that my taking a cottage at the very end of it is rather wondered at than approved. But I feel very safe, because I believe no one robs or kills without temptation or provocation, and as I have nothing to tempt thieves, so I am determined not to provoke murderers.

My house is one of the better kind of really Chilian cottages. It consists of a little entrance-hall, and a large sitting-room sixteen feet square, at one end of which a door opens into a little dark bedroom, and a door in the hall opens into another a little less. This is the body of the house, in front of which, looking to the south-west, there is a broad veranda. Adjoining, there is a servant's room, and at a little distance the kitchen.

My landlord, who deals in horses, has stables for them and his oxen, and several small cottages for his peons* and their families, besides storehouses all around.

There is a garden in front of the house, which slopes down towards the little river that divides me from the Almendral, stored with apples, pears, almonds, peaches, grapes, oranges, olives, and quinces, besides pumpkins, melons, cabbages, potatoes, French beans, and maize, and a few flowers, and behind the house the barest reddest hill in the neighbourhood rises pretty abruptly. It affords earth for numerous beautiful shrubs, and is worn in places by the constant tread of the mules, who bring firewood, charcoal, and vegetables, to the Valparaiso market.

The interior of the house is clean, the walls are whitewashed, and the roof is planked, for stucco ceilings would not stand the frequent earthquakes, of which we had one pretty smart shock to-night.

No Valparaiso native house of the middling class boasts more than one window, and that is not glazed, but generally secured by carved wooden or iron lattice-work. This is, of course, in the public sitting-room, so that the bedrooms are perfectly dark.

I am considered fortunate in having doors to mine, but there is none between the hall and sitting-room, so I have made bold to hang up a curtain, to the wonder of my landlady, who cannot understand my finding no amusement in watching the motions of the servants or visitors who may be in the outer room.

May 10th

Thanks to my friends both ashore and in the frigate, I am now

* Day labourers.

pretty comfortably settled in my little *home*. Every body has been kind. One neighbour lends me a horse, another such furniture as I require. Nation and habits make no difference. I arrived here in need of kindness, and I have received it from all.

I have great comfort in strolling on the hill behind my house, it commands a lovely view of the port and neighbouring hills. It is totally uncultivated, and in the best season can afford but poor browsing for mules or horses. . . . The red soil of my hill is crossed here and there by great ridges of white half marble, half sparry stone, and all its sides bear deep marks of winter torrents. In the beds of these I have found pieces of green stone of a soft soapy appearance, and lumps of quartz and coarse granite. One of these water-courses was once worked for gold, but the quantity found was so inconsiderable, that the proprietor was glad to quit the precarious adventure, and to cultivate the chacra or garden-ground which joins to mine, and whose produce has been much more beneficial to his family.

I went to walk in that garden, and found there, besides the fruits common to my own, figs, lemons, and pomegranates, and the hedges full of white cluster roses. The mistress of the house is a near relation of my landlady, and takes in washing, but that by no means implies that either her rank or her pretensions are as low as those of an European washerwoman.

Her mother was possessed of no less than eight chacras, but as she is ninety years old, that must have been a hundred years ago, when Valparaiso was by no means so large a place, and consequently chacras were less valuable. However, she was a great proprietor of land, but as is usual here, most of it went to portion off a large family of daughters, and some I am afraid to pay the expenses of the gold found on the estate.

The old lady, seeing me in the garden, courteously invited me to walk in. The veranda in front of the house is like my own, paved with bricks nine inches square, and supported by rude wooden pillars, which the Chileno architects fancy they have carved handsomely. I found under it two of the most beautiful boys I ever saw, and a very pretty young woman, the grandchildren of the old lady.

They all got up from the bench eager to receive me, and show me kindness. One of the boys ran to fetch his mother, the other went to gather a bunch of roses for me, and the daughter Joanita, taking me into the house gave me some beautiful carnations.

From the garden we entered immediately into the common sitting-room, where, according to custom, one low latticed window afforded but a scanty light. . . . On a table in a corner, under a glass case, I saw a little religious baby work, – a waxen Jesus an inch long, sprawls on a waxen Virgin's knee, surrounded by Joseph, the oxen and asses, all of the same goodly material, decorated with moss and sea shells.

Near this I observed a pot of beautiful flowers, and two pretty-shaped silver utensils, which I at first took for implements of worship, and then for inkstands, but I discovered that one was a little censer for burning pastile, with which the young women perfume their handkerchiefs and mantos, and the other the vase for holding the infusion of the herb of Paraguay, commonly called matte, so universally drank or rather sucked here.

The herb appears like dried senna; a small quantity of it is put into the little vase with a proportion of sugar, and sometimes a bit of lemon peel, the water is poured boiling on it, and it is instantly sucked up through a tube about six inches long. This is the great luxury of the Chilenos, both male and female. . . . I have not yet tasted of it, and do not much relish the idea of using the same tube with a dozen other people. . . .

11th May

This morning, tempted by the exceeding fineness of the weather, and the sweet feeling of the air, I set out to follow the little water-course that irrigates my garden, towards its source.

After skirting the hill for about a furlong, always looking down on a fertile valley, and now and then gaining a peep at the bay and shipping between the fruit trees, I heard the sound of falling water, and on turning sharp round the corner of a rock, I found myself in a quebrada, or ravine, full of great blocks of granite, from which a bright plentiful stream had washed the red clay as it leaped down from ledge to ledge, and fell into a little bed of sand glistening with particles of mica that looked like fairy gold. . . .

Among the humble flowers I remarked varieties of our common garden herbs, carraway, fennel, sage, thyme, mint, rue, wild carrot, and several sorts of sorrel. But it is not yet the season of flowers. Here and there only, a solitary fuscia or andromeda was to be found – but I did not want flowers – the very feel of the open air, the verdure, the sunshine, were enough, and I doubly enjoyed this my first rural walk after being so long at sea.

Friday, May 17th

Three days of half fog, half rain, have given notice of the breaking up of the dry season, and my landlord has accordingly sent people to prepare the roof for the coming wet weather. . . .

Returning from a short walk to-day, I had a good opportunity of seeing a group of horsemen, young and old, who had come from the neighbourhood of Rancagua, a town near the foot of the Andes, to the southward of Santiago, with a cargo of wine and brandy.

The liquor is contained in skins, and brought from the interior on mules. It is not uncommon to see a hundred and fifty of these under the guidance of ten or a dozen peons, with the guaso or farmer at their head, encamping in some open spot near a farm-house in the neighbourhood of the town. Many of these houses keep spare buildings, in which their itinerant friends secure their liquor while they go to the farms around, or even into town, to seek customers, not choosing to pay the heavy toll for going into the port, unless certain of sale for the wine.

I bought a quantity for common use. It is a rich, strong, and sweetish white wine, capable, with good management, of great improvement, and infinitely preferable to any of the Cape wines, excepting Constantia, that I ever drank. I gave six dollars for two arobas of it, so that it comes to about 3½d. per bottle. . . .

18th

One of my young friends from the *Doris*, some of whom have been with me daily, has brought me some excellent partridges of his own shooting. They are somewhat larger than the partridges in England, but I think quite as good, when properly dressed, or rather plucked, but the cooks here have a habit of scalding the feathers off, which hurts the flavour of the bird.

There are several kinds of birds here good to eat, but neither quail nor pheasant. They have plenty of enemies, from the condor, through every variety of the eagle, vulture, hawk, and owl, down to the ugly, dull, green parrot of Chile, which never looks tolerably well, except on the wing, and then the under part, of purple and yellow, is handsome. The face is peculiarly ugly, his parrot's beak being set in so close as to be to other parrots what the pug dog is to a greyhound.

They are great foes to the little singing birds, whose notes as well as plumage resemble those of the linnet, and which abound in this neighbourhood. We have also a kind of blackbird with a soft, sweet, but very low note, a saucy thing that repeats two notes only, not unlike the mockbird, and that never moves out of the way. Swallows and humming-birds are plenty, and the boys* tell me they have seen marvellous storks and cranes in the marshes, which I shall take occasion to visit after the rains. . . .

Monday, May 20th

This is but a sad day. The *Doris* sailed early, and I feel again alone in the world. In her are gone the only relation, the only acquaintance I have in this wide country. In parting between friends, those who go have always less to feel than those who remain. . . .

In the course of the day, however, the kindly acts and expressions of my new neighbours, and the friendly attentions of Commodore and Mrs Stewart of the American line-of-battle ship *Franklin*, of Baron Macau of His Catholic Majesty's ship *Clorinde*, and others, both English and foreigners, persuade me that there are yet many kindly hearts around me, and check the regrets I might otherwise indulge in.

Yet I cannot forget that I am a widow, unprotected, and in a foreign land, separated from all my natural friends by distant and dangerous ways, whether I return by sea or land!

22d

We have news from Peru, for the first time since my arrival, I think. A body of General San Martin's army has been surprised, and destroyed by the royalists. The Chileno squadron, under Lord Cochrane, has returned to Callao, from its dangerous and difficult voyage to Acapulco, after chasing the two last remaining Spanish ships into patriot ports, where they have been forced to surrender, and it is said that San Martin has offered most flattering terms of reconciliation to Lord Cochrane.

If I understand matters aright, it may be possible for His Lordship to listen to them, for the sake of the cause, but, personally, he will surely never repose the slightest confidence in him.

The tragi-comedy of the vexed relationship between General San Martin and Lord Cochrane was now drawing to its close.

* The midshipmen of the *Doris*.

Between 1819 and 1822 these two remarkable men had successfully challenged the colonial Spanish on land and sea, thereby ensuring the continued independence of Chile, the cutting out of the Spanish flag in the Pacific, and the eventual liberation of Peru. Yet, like Tweedle-Dum and Tweedle-Dee, they had disagreed in almost everything, from the way the war should be conducted, to the constitution that should be set up once Peru was liberated. Above all they had disagreed over the pay, maintenance and employment of the Chilean navy of which Lord Cochrane was admiral. And on their differences the hotch-potch of adventurers who surrounded each man maliciously and successfully played.

Their widely differing personalities continue to exercise the judgment of historians even now, as they puzzled and infuriated contemporaries then, including Maria Graham herself. And it is one of the few flaws in her otherwise precise and fair-minded interpretation of events that while justly appreciating the excellencies of her friend, Lord Cochrane, she should in common with many of the English have allowed her judgment to be clouded by contemporary unjust reflections on San Martin. Though, as will be seen, when she came to meet the man she found him attractive in spite of herself.

The clashes between the two men seem to have been largely caused by a differing style and temperament; San Martin secretive, suave, biding his time, with a concealed idealism, even a trace of mysticism; Lord Cochrane extrovert, dashing, and, though unquestionably in the adventure for what he could get out of it, idealistic after his own fashion, and a bitter enemy to all but his own autocracy.

Maria's journal entry of 22 May alludes to what was certainly San Martin's final attempt at a reconciliation, during which he proposed appointing Cochrane admiral over the joint squadrons of Peru and Chile, and held out the opportunity of acquiring immense wealth should Cochrane lend his help in securing the Philippine Islands, the proposition topped by the offer of the showy diamond star of the Order of Merit. All to be summarily rejected by the admiral, who declared with passion that he would not accept office, titles or honours, from a government founded on the breach of that faith which had promised the free choice of constitution to the people of Peru, and which was supported by tyranny, oppression, and the violation of all laws.

This drama had occurred at about the time Maria landed in Valparaiso, though six weeks before an aide of San Martin's had sent a file of accusations against Lord Cochrane to the Chilean government. Whether San Martin knew of his aide's initiative is uncertain, though the accusations, Maria tells us, were unfounded, proof of which was contained in documents held at Santiago.

23d

To-day, for the first time since I came *home*, I rode to the port, and had leisure to observe the shops, markets, and wharf, if one may give that name to the platform before the custom-house.

The native shops, though very small, appear to me generally cleaner than those of Portuguese America. The silks of China, France, and Italy, the printed cottons of Britain, rosaries, amulets, and glass from Germany – generally furnish them. The stuffs of the country are very seldom to be purchased in a shop, because few are made but for domestic consumption. . . .

The English shops are more numerous than any. Hardware, pottery, and cotton and woollen cloths, form of course the staple articles. It is amusing to observe the ingenuity with which the Birmingham artists have accommodated themselves to the coarse transatlantic tastes. The framed saints, the tinsel snuff-boxes, the gaudy furniture, make one smile when contrasted with the decent and elegant simplicity of these things in Europe.

The Germans furnish most of the glass in common use. It is of bad quality to be sure, but it, as well as the little German mirrors, which are chiefly brought to hang up as votive offerings in the chapels, answers all the purposes of Chileno consumption. . . .

English tailors, shoemakers, saddlers, and inn-keepers, hang out their signs in every street, and the preponderance of the English language over every other spoken in the chief streets, would make one fancy Valparaiso a coast town in Britain.

The North Americans greatly assist in this, however. Their goods, consisting of common furniture, flour, biscuit, and naval stores, necessarily keep them busier out of doors than any other set of people. The more elegant Parisian or London furniture is generally despatched unopened to Santiago, where the demand for articles of mere luxury is of course greater. The number of piano-fortes brought from England is astonishing. There is scarcely a house without one, as the fondness for music is excessive; and many of the young ladies play with skill and taste, though few take the trouble to learn the gamut,* but trust entirely to the ear. . . .

Returning from my shopping, I stopped at the apothecary's (for there is but one), to buy some powder-blue, which, to my surprise, I found could only be procured there. I fancy it must resemble an apothecary's of the fourteenth century, for it is even more antique looking than those I have seen in Italy or France.

* Scale.

The man has a taste for natural history, so that besides his jars of old-fashioned medicines, inscribed all over with the celestial signs, oddly intermixed with packets of patent medicines from London, dried herbs, and filthy gallipots, there are fishes' heads and snakes' skins. In one corner a great condor tearing the flesh from the bones of a lamb, in another a monster sheep, having an adscititious* leg growing from the skin of his forehead, and there are chickens, and cats, and parrots, altogether producing a combination of antique dust and recent filth, far exceeding any thing I ever beheld. . . .

May 30th

I dined to-day in the port, with my very kind friends, Mr Hogan, the American consul, and his wife and daughters. . . .

I had an opportunity to-day of observing how carelessly even sensible men make their observations in foreign countries, and on daily matters concerning them. A physician, at dinner, mentioned the medicinal qualities of the culen (*Cytisus Arboreus*), and that it would be worth while to bring it into Chile, or at least to the neighbourhood of Valparaiso, to cultivate, for the purpose of exportation. I was almost afraid to say, as I am a new-comer, that the country people had shown me a plant they called culen, but, on venturing to tell the gentleman so, he said it could not be because he never heard of it here.

I went home, walked to the Quebrada, found the rocks on both sides covered with the best culen, and the inferior sort which grows much higher, not uncommon. Yet he is a clever man, and has resided some years in the country. This same culen is very agreeable as tea, and is said to possess antiscorbutic and antifebrile qualities, the smell of the dried leaves is pleasant, and a sweetish gum exudes from the flower-stalks. This gum is used by shoemakers instead of wax; and the fresh leaves, formed into a salve with hogs'-lard, are applied with good effect to recent wounds. . . .

Friday, May 31st

To-day I indulged myself with a walk which I had been wishing to take for some days, to an obscure portion of the Almendral, called the Rincona, or nook, I suppose because it is in a little corner formed by two projecting hills. My object in going thither was to

* Extra.

see the manufactory of coarse pottery, which I supposed to be established there, because I was told that the *ollas*, or jars, for cooking and carrying water, the earthen lamps, and the earthen braziers, were all made there. . . . I found the Rincona beyond some ruined but thick walls, which stretch from the foot of the hills to the sea, and which were once intended as a defence to the port on that side. They are nothing now.

I looked round in vain for any thing large enough either to be a manufactory, or even to contain the necessary furnaces for baking the pottery, nevertheless I passed many huts, at the doors of which I saw jars and dishes set out for sale, and concluded that these were the huts of the inferior workmen. However, on advancing a little farther I found that I must look for no regular manufactory, no division of labour, no machinery, not even the potter's wheel, none of the aids to industry which I had conceived almost indispensable to a trade so artificial as that of making earthenware.

At the door of one of the poorest huts, formed merely of branches and covered with long grass, having a hide for a door, sat a family of manufacturers. They were seated on sheep-skins spread under the shade of a little penthouse formed of green boughs, at their work. A mass of clay ready tempered lay before them, and each person according to age and ability was forming jars, plates, or dishes. The work-people were all women, and I believe that no man condescends to employ himself in this way, that is, in making the small ware, the large wine jars, &c. of Melipilla are made by men.

As the shortest way of learning is to mix at once with those we wish to learn from, I seated myself on the sheep-skin and began to work too, imitating as I could a little girl who was making a simple saucer. The old woman who seemed the chief directress, looked at me very gravely, and then took my work and showed me how to begin it anew, and work its shape aright.

All this, to be sure, I might have guessed at, but the secret I wanted to learn, was the art of polishing the clay, for it is not rendered shining by any of the glazing processes I have seen, therefore I waited patiently and worked at my dish till it was ready. Then the old woman put her hand into a leathern pocket which she wore in front, and drew out a smooth shell, with which she first formed the edges and borders anew, and then rubbed it, first gently, and, as the clay hardened, with great force, dipping the shell occasionally in water, all over the surface, until a perfect polish was produced, and the vessel was set to dry in the shade. . . .

It is impossible to conceive a greater degree of apparent poverty than is exhibited in the potters' cottages of the Rincona. Most, however, had a decent bed. A few stakes driven into the ground, and laced across with thongs, form the bedstead. A mattress of wool, and, where the women are industrious, sheets of coarse homespun cotton and thick woollen coverlets form no contemptible resting-place for the man and wife, or rather for the wife, for I believe the men pass the greater part of every night, according to the custom of the country, sleeping, wrapped up in their ponchos, in the open air.

The infants are hung in little hammocks of sheep-skin to the poles of the roof, and the other children or relations sleep as they can on skins, wrapped in their ponchos, on the ground.

In one of the huts there was no bed, the whole furniture consisted of two skin trunks, and there were eleven inhabitants, including two infants, twins, there being neither father nor man of any kind to own or protect them.

The natural gentleness and goodness of nature of the people of Chile preserve even the vicious, at least among the women, from that effrontery which such a family as I here visited would, and must, have exhibited in Europe.

My instructress had a husband, and her house was more decent. It had a bed, it had a raised bench formed of clay, and there were the implements of female industry, a distaff and spindle, and knitting needles formed of the spines of the great torch-thistle from Coquimbo, which grow to nine inches long. But the hamlet of the Rincona is the most wretched I have yet seen.

Its natives, however, pointed out to me their beautiful view, which is indeed magnificent, across the ocean to the snow-capped Andes, and boasted of the pleasure of walking on their hills on a holiday evening. Then they showed me their sweet and wholesome stream of water, and their ancient fig-trees, inviting me to go back 'when the figs should be ripe, and the flowers looking at themselves in the stream'.

I was ashamed of some of the expressions of pity that had escaped me. – If I cannot better their condition, why awaken them to a sense of its miseries?

It was twilight long before I reached home, and the evening had become chill and gloomy, and I sat down in my solitary cottage, and thought of the hopes and wishes with which I had left England, and almost doubted whether I, too, had not passed the bounds of life.

But such abstractions can never happily last long. The ordinary current of existence rolls not so smoothly, but that at every turn some inequality awakens consciousness, and I roused myself to my daily task of study, and of writing down the occurrences of the day. . . .

June 2d

A rainy morning, and feeling cold, yet the thermometer not below 50° of Fahrenheit. While I was at breakfast, one of my little neighbours came running in, screaming out 'Señora, he is come! he is come!'

'Who is come, child?'

'Our admiral, our great and good admiral; and if you come to the veranda, you will see the flags in the Almendral.'

Accordingly, I looked out, and did see the Chilian flag hoisted at every door: and two ships more in the roads* than there were yesterday. The *O'Higgins* and *Valdivia* had arrived during the night, and all the inhabitants of the port and suburbs had made haste to display their flags and their joy on Lord Cochrane's safe return.

I am delighted at his arrival, not only because I want to see him, whom I look up to as my natural friend here,† but because I think he ought to have influence to mend some things, and to prevent others, which, without such influence, will, I fear, prove highly detrimental to the rising state of Chile, if not to the general cause of South American independence. . . .

What concerned Maria was the new and ostensibly more representative constitution that O'Higgins, the Chilean Director, was currently drafting in response to criticism of the illiberal nature of his government.

'I am too old not to be afraid of ready-made constitutions,' she wrote with an insight curiously relevant to-day, 'and especially of one fitted to the habits of a highly civilized people applied too suddenly to an infant nation like this.'[1]

In the event O'Higgins took care that the new constitution should be drafted in such a way that his indefinite continuation in office was virtually guaranteed. Yet within the year he was to be superseded in the Directorship.

---

* A stretch of water where ships ride at anchor.
† Captain Graham had been a midshipman on Lord Cochrane's ship, the *Thetis*.

June 6th

To-day the feast of the Corpus Domini was celebrated and I went to the Iglesia Matriz with my friend Mrs Campbell to hear her brother Don Mariano de Escalada preach.

We went at 9 o'clock, she had put off her French or English dress, and adopted the Spanish costume, I did so also, so far as to wear a mantilla instead of a bonnet, such being the custom on going to church. A boy followed us with missals, and a carpet to kneel on.

The church, like all other buildings here, appears mean from without, but within it is large and decently decorated. To be sure the Virgin was in white satin, with a hoop and silver fringes, surrounded with looking-glasses, and supported on either hand by St Peter and St Paul, the former in a lace cassock, and the latter in a robe formed of the same block which composes his own gracious personage.

As there was to be a procession, and as the governor was to be a principal person in the ceremonies preceding it, we waited his arrival for the beginning of the service until 11 o'clock, so that I had plenty of time to look at the church, the saints, and the ladies, who were, generally speaking, very pretty, and becomingly dressed with their mantillas and braided hair.

At length the great man arrived, and it was whispered that he had been transacting business with the admiral,* and transmitting to him, and the captains, and other officers, the thanks of the government for their services. But the whispers died away, and the young preacher began.

The sermon was of course occasional.† It spoke in good language of the moral freedom conferred by the Christian dispensation, and thence the step was not far to political freedom. But the argument was so decorously managed, that it could offend none, and yet so strongly urged that it might persuade many. I was highly pleased with it. . . . The procession was now arranged; and my friend and I, to escape joining it, hurried out of church, and took a stand to see it at some distance. . . .

There was a pretty part of the show . . . on the water. About a hundred and fifty little boats and canoes, dressed with the national colours, and firing rockets every now and then, rowed round the bay, and stopped at every church, and before every fishing cove, to sing a hymn, or chaunt.

* Lord Cochrane.
† i.e. for this particular occasion.

After accompanying them for some time, I went into Mr Hoseason's house, and there I found Lord Cochrane. I should say he looks better than when I last saw him in England, although his life of exertion and anxiety has not been such as is in general favourable to the looks. – How my heart yearned to think that when our own country lost his service, England,

> Like a base Ethiope, threw a pearl away
> Richer than all his kind.*

But he is doing honour to his native land, by supporting that cause which used to be hers, and in after-ages his name will be among those of the household gods of the Chilenos.

On Lord Cochrane's arrival here from Lima, every body was of course anxious to hear what he, and the officers of the squadron in general, think and feel concerning the protectorate of Peru.

His Lordship, however, does not say any thing concerning the conduct of San Martin, but the officers are not so discreet. They universally represent the present government of Peru as most despotic and tyrannical, now and then stained by cruelties more like the frenetic acts of the Czar Paul than the inflictions of even the greatest military tyrants. . . .

There is now in this port a vessel, the *Milagro*, full of Spanish prisoners, to whom San Martin had promised security and protection for their persons and property. However, after paying half their property for letters of naturalization, and for permission to retain the rest, and with it to leave Lima, they were seized and stripped on the road to Callao, huddled on board the prison-ship, and are now in the bay to be sent to the rest of the prisoners at Santiago, whose captivity is too probably for life, as they are only to be liberated when Old Spain acknowledges the independence of her colonies.

These poor people have arrived without the common necessaries of life, and leave has been refused to supply some of their most pressing wants – but Lord Cochrane has done it without leave. Would that he could inspire these people with some of the humanities of war as practised in Europe!

8th

I went to pay a visit to the wife of my landlord, who had often entreated me to go and take matee with her, but my dread of using

---

* Lord Cochrane had led a brilliant though (owing to his volatile temperament) chequered career in the Royal Navy.

the bombilla, or tube which passes round to every body for the purpose of sucking it up, had hitherto deterred me. However, I resolved to get over my prejudice, and accordingly walked to her house this evening. . . .

In the entrance-hall the servants were sitting, or standing loitering, for the working time of day was over. They were looking into the family apartment, where the women were lolling on the estrada, or raised platform covered with carpet (alfombra), supported by cushions, on one side of the room, the men, with their hats on, were sitting on high chairs, smoking and spitting, on the other. Along the wall by the estrada, a covered bench runs the whole length of the room, and there I was invited to sit, and the matee was called for.

A relation of the lady then went to the lower end of the estrada, and sat on the edge of it, before a large chafingdish of lighted charcoal, on which was a copper-pot full of boiling water. The matee cups were then handed to the matee maker, who, after putting in the proper ingredients, poured the boiling water over them, applied the bombilla to her lips, and then handed it to me. But it was long ere I could venture to taste the boiling liquor, which is harsher than tea, but still very pleasant.

As soon as I had finished my cup, it was instantly replenished and handed to another person, and so on till all were served, two cups and tubes having gone round the whole circle. Soon after the matee, sugar-biscuits were handed round, and then cold water, which concluded the visit.

The people I went to see were of the better class of shopkeepers, dignified by the name of merchants, and holding a small landed estate under one of the mayorasgos near the chacra where I reside. Their manners are decent, and there is a grace and kindliness in the women that might adorn the most polished drawing-rooms, and which prevents the want of education from being so disgusting as in our own country, where it is generally accompanied by vulgarity.

Here the want of cultivation sends women back to their natural means of persuasion, gentleness and caresses, and if a little cunning mingles with them, it is the protection nature has given the weak against the strong.

In England a pretty ignorant woman is nine times in ten a vixen, and rules or tries to rule accordingly. Here the simplicity of nature approaches to the highest refinements of education, and a well-born and well-bred English gentlewoman is not very different in external manners from a Chilena girl.

June 12th

After three days' rain, this morning is as fine 'as that on which Paradise was created'. So I spent half of it in gardening, half in wandering about the quebradas in search of wild flowers. First, in the sandy lane near me I found a variety of the yellow horned poppy, and the common mallow of England, besides the cultivated variety with pink flowers; vervain, two or three kinds of trefoil, fumitory, fennel, pimpernel, and a small scarlet mallow with flowers not larger. These, with three or four geraniums, sorrel, dock, the ribbed plantain, lucerne, which is the common fodder here, and several other small flowers, made me imagine myself in an English lane. . . .

19 June – 24 August 1822

Wednesday, June 19th

These few last days I have been less alone. My friend Miss H. is staying with me, and we have had many pleasant walks together; and I have become acquainted with several of the Chileno naval officers.

Captain Foster, who was the senior captain, has given up his command, and, it is said, has tendered his resignation to the supreme government. He very kindly came the other day to superintend the putting up a stove in my little sitting-room.

I have hitherto used an open brasier, but, though very comfortable, the fumes of the charcoal must be hurtful, but with a stove, they pass off through the funnel. Several houses have now English stoves and grates, but the burning of coal is not yet very general. English coal is of course dear, and the coal from the province of Conception, which resembles the Scotch coal, is not yet worked to a sufficient extent to supply the market.

Of the officers actually belonging to the squadron, I have seen Captain Crosbie, Lord Cochrane's flag captain, a pleasant gentleman-like young Irishman, brave as Lord Cochrane's captain ought to be, and intelligent.

Captain Cobbet, the nephew of Cobbet,* with a great deal of the hard-headed sense of his uncle, and also (if all physiognomical presages are not false), endowed with no small share of his selfishness, owes every thing, education and promotion, both in the English navy and this,† to Lord Cochrane, and has the reputation of being an excellent seaman. I find him polite, intelligent, and communicative. But the person who seems peculiarly to possess the information concerning all I want to know, is the physician of the *O'Higgins*, Dr Craig. Skill in his profession, good sense, rational curiosity, and enthusiasm of character concealed under a shy exterior, render him a more interesting person than ninety-nine in a hundred to be met with on this side of Cape Horn, and I feel peculiarly happy in making his acquaintance.

* William Cobbett (1763–1835) radical journalist and author of *Rural Rides*.
† The Chilean navy.

It is not unpleasant to have one's solitude now and then broken in upon by persons who, like these, have characters of their own, but there is a sad proportion in the English society here of trash.

However, as vulgarity, ignorance, and coarseness, often disguise kindness of heart, and as I have experienced the latter from all, it scarcely becomes me to complain of the roughness of the coat of the pineapple while enjoying the flavour of the fruit. . . .

20th

To-day, being anxious to procure a variety of scene for my young friend,* we walked to what is usually called the flower-garden here, and I, at least, highly enjoyed the day.

On reaching the house of the mistress of the garden, we found her seated on the brick bench before the door. She appears very old, her hair, which fell in a single braid down her back, being perfectly grey. She is tall and hale-looking, and soon summoned three of her five daughters to receive us. The youngest of these appeared to be at least fifty, tall, muscular, well made, with the remains of decided beauty, with an elastic step and agreeable voice. They stepped forward bearing carpets for us to sit on, and oranges to refresh us. The other two, of scarcely less imposing appearance, joined us, and invited us to walk into the garden. . . . On returning to the house . . . we found our old lady sitting where we had left her, distributing advice and plants of various kinds to two or three women and children, who had collected round her while we were in the garden . . .

Among the little girls were two fishermen's children with laver, another sort of sea-weed, and several kinds of shell-fish for sale, some of which I had never seen before. Upon my saying so, my young companion and I were asked to come some day to eat of them dressed in the country fashion. It was too late to-day to prepare any, but we were so earnestly pressed to come back after our intended walk to the Quebrada, farther on, and partake of the family dinner, that I, loving to see all things, readily consented, and accordingly returned at two o'clock to the flower-garden house.

We found the mother sitting alone on the estrada, supported by her cushions, with a small low round table before her, on which was spread a cotton cloth, by no means clean. The daughters only

* Miss H.

served their mother, but ate their own meals in the kitchen by the fire. We were accommodated with seats at the old lady's table.

The first dish that appeared was a small platter of melted marrow, into which we were invited to dip the bread that had been presented to each, the old lady setting the example, and even presenting bits thoroughly sopped, with her fingers, to Miss H., who contrived to pass them on to a puppy who sat behind her. I, not being so near, escaped better, besides, as I really did not dislike the marrow, though I wished in vain for the addition of pepper and salt, I dipped my bread most diligently, and ate heartily. . . . After this *apetizer*, as my countrymen would call it, a large dish of charqui-can was placed before us. It consists of fresh beef very much boiled, with pieces of charqui or dried beef, slices of dried tongue, and pumkin, cabbage, potatoes, and other vegetables, in the same dish.

Our hostess immediately began eating from the dish with her fingers, and invited us to do the same, but one of her daughters brought us each a plate and fork, saying she knew that such was our custom. However, the old lady persisted in putting delicate pieces on our plates with her thumb and finger.

The dish was good, and well cooked. It was succeeded by a fowl which was torn to pieces with the hands, and then came another fowl cut up, and laid on sippets* strewed with chopped herbs, and then giblets, and then soup, and lastly, a bowl of milk, and a plate of *Harina de Yalli*, that is, flour made from a small and delicate kind of maize. Each being served with a cup of the milk, we stirred the flour into it, and I thought it excellent from its resemblance to milk brose.

Our drink was the wine of the country, and on going out to the veranda after dinner, apples and oranges were offered to us.

As it was not yet time for the old lady to take her siesta, I took the opportunity of asking her concerning the belief of the people of the country as to witches. There is something in her appearance, when surrounded by her five tall daughters, that irresistibly put me in mind of the weird sisters . . . my hostess could not have looked more shocked. She crossed herself, took up the scapulary† of the Merced, which she kissed, and then said,

'There have been such things as witches, but it would be mortal sin to believe or consult them, from which, may our lady defend me and mine,' and little more was to be got from her on that subject, though she launched out at great length into a history of

* Morsels of bread.
† The receipt for payment for right of burial in the consecrated ground of the Merced.

saints and miracles, wrought particularly against the heretics, especially the Russians, in favour of the faithful Spaniards.

I find, however, that witches here do much the same things as in Europe; they influence the birth of animals, nay, even of children; spoil milk, wither trees, and control the winds. . . .

The superstitions and the cookery of to-day are both decidedly Spanish, though some of the materials for both are aboriginal Americans, no bad type, I fancy, of the character of the nation.

24th, St John's day

The balmy *nucca* drop* of the midnight, between the eve of St John and this day, seems to have fallen here, all is gay and idle, every body walking about in holyday-clothes.

I am sorry, however, to find that the time of the Spaniards† is talked of with some little lingering regret. The present government, by suppressing a great many of the religious shows, has certainly relieved the people from a heavy tax, but then it has curtailed their accustomed amusements. In a climate such as this, where constant labour is not necessary to support life, some consideration ought to be had to the necessity of amusement for those classes, especially where purely mental entertainment is nothing. The festival of St Peter, peculiarly adapted to a maritime place, should not, I think, have been abolished. . . .

Chile is so obviously a maritime country, shut up as she is to landward, by the Andes from the eastern provinces, and the desert of Atacama from those to the north, that I would, were I its legislator, turn every feeling and passion towards the sea.

St Peter's day should be a national and naval spectacle. I would distribute prizes to fishermen and boatmen. I would bestow honorary rewards on officers. I would receive and answer petitions and representations from all connected with the sea. In short, I would, on that day, let them feel that the protection of government went hand in hand with that of religion over the most useful, and therefore the most favoured class of Chileno citizens. . . .

27th

I paid a visit to Madame Zenteno the governor's lady, a pleasing, lively little woman, who received me very politely, and sent for her

* The drop which falls from heaven, and stops the plague in Egypt.
† Before Chile was independent.

husband, who came immediately, and seemed delighted to display the English comforts of the apartment I was received in.

An English carpet, an English grate, and even English coals, were all very agreeable on this cold raw day. Zenteno assured me that he found a fire thus burned in an open stove was the best promoter of conversation, and regretted the many years he had passed without even guessing at its comforts. He is properly anxious to promote a taste for the elegancies of civilized life, but under any other circumstances, I should say that there was even a little affectation in his great admiration for everything English.

However, the people of Valparaiso are indebted to him for considerable improvements in the roads and streets, and a plan for a new market-place, as soon as the funds will permit, is to be carried into execution. These things seem little to Europeans. But they forget that this Valparaiso, one of the greatest ports on this side of the vast continent of South America, is little more in appearance than an English fishing town. SIDMOUTH is a capital city in comparison.

From the governor's house I went to the jail, a strong uncomfortable building now empty. The prisoners are transferred to the hospital of San Juan de Dios, and I am ashamed to say the Spanish prisoners from Lima, sent by San Martin, are there also, along with the common felons. The Spaniards were in so wretched a condition on their arrival, that the English inhabitants, in order to save them from starving, have raised a subscription; and one of the merchants daily sees their food distributed.

29th

To-day three hundred of the prisoners from Lima were sent off to Santiago, some on foot, and others, whose age and infirmities rendered it impossible for them to march, in waggons. Among the latter, one old man with thin grey hair was seated, and was heard to apostrophize the sea, whose shores he was leaving, as the only road to his native country. Feebly lamenting, he sat carelessly on the edge of the vehicle, when, just as it turned to go up the first cuesta, he fell and died on the spot, – it was not of the fall, but of a broken heart. His companions say, that, with the word Spain on his lips, he died in the cart and then fell. . . .

It is the festival of Nuestra Señora del Pilar *La Avogada de los Marineros*.* How could I do otherwise than observe it?

* The protector of seamen.

I went to my old friend at the flower-garden, who is commonly called La Chavelita, and, as I knew she intended being at the ceremony which takes place at the church of the Merced, I obtained permission to accompany her, and the afternoon was productive of considerable amusement and information, which I could not have obtained without such a companion.

In the first place, I do not know if I should otherwise ever have had courage to go into a ventana or wine-house, which I did to-day. We arrived at the church-door too early, and, after walking up and down the space proposed for the procession, we went to the said ventana, which is exactly opposite to the church. I imagined, at first, that it was a private house belonging to a friend of La Chavelita, and the table at the door set out with fruit and cakes for sale, seemed to me to be only a compliment to the festival.

On entering a very large room, with benches round three sides and a brassero in the middle, I saw on the fourth side of the apartment, a table covered with jugs and bottles, containing various kinds of liquor, and glasses of different sizes by them. On one of the benches sat two religious of the order of the Merced, with their long, full, white robes with black crosses and enormous hats, smoking and talking politics. . . . Our entrance interrupted them for an instant, when, after a few minutes whispering, in which I now and then heard the words *Vinda Inglez*, they resumed their politics, and then, having finished their segars, walked out.

Meantime I had observed several elderly fat women running about, and mixing various liquors, and carrying them into several inner apartments. Some of these liquors I tasted. Little spirits or wine was called for, but several kinds of sherbet, the best of which is Luca, were in great request. The Luca, is an infusion of culen and canela (*wild cinnamon*), with a little syrup, and is said to be as wholesome as it is pleasant.

The house shortly began to fill. Company after company of young men arrived, and were shown into different rooms, and I then found out where I was.*

Some parties called for dinners of so many dishes, others for wine, some for sweet drinks and cakes, and music, and all for segars.

Some good-looking girls now made their appearance, and with guitars entered the rooms where music had been ordered. Soon we heard the sound of singing and dancing, and I was quite satisfied

---

* Is this remark intentionally cryptic?

that every body was happy and merry, and left the place, persuaded that the evening would be still gayer, . . .

It was now time, however, to repair to the church. And there, kneeling before the high altar, we heard the Mass to our lady of the glittering brow, and prayed for the safety of the living seamen, and for the souls of those who were gone.

I cannot and I will not think it unlawful to join in such prayers, and I never felt my devotion more fervent. But I was soon roused from it to join in the procession, and then, indeed, I felt my Protestant prejudices return.

Our lady was taken out dressed in brown satin, and jewels of value, and carried towards the sea, through a lane formed of boughs of green myrtle and bay. Here and there was a shrine at which she stopped, and a chaunt was sung. Then, having thus visited San Josef, Santa Dolores, and Santa Geltrudes, she was carried back at sunset to her own altar, and the Ave Maria Stella was sung. . . .

July 1st

Late last night His Majesty's ship *Alacrity* came in from Lima, and brought me letters from my friends of the *Doris*. She also brought intelligence concerning Lima, which confirms all that we have heard of the hateful though plausible San Martin.

It is well known that the merchant Don Pedro Abadia, besides being one of the richest merchants in South America, was also one of the most enlightened, liberal, and respectable men. For this excellent person San Martin had always professed the greatest friendship, and made use of his knowledge and talents in the regulation of his custom-houses and his taxes. But having obtained his end thus far, the riches of Abadia excited his cupidity, and he proceeded by the basest treachery to procure an excuse for arresting him.

Knowing that an immense property of Abadia's was in the hands of the royalists at Pasco, San Martin instructed two monks to go to him and offer to convey such letters to the commanders of the Spanish troops as might, at least, prevent the absolute ruin of the property, which chiefly consisted in mines, and in most expensive machinery which he had imported from England, with the idea and the hope of improving the country by the introduction of such machinery into it.

The monks of course betrayed Abadia. He was thrown into prison, and tried before a tribunal instituted by San Martin. Yet, as his letters had been strictly confined to the business of his estates and machinery, he was acquitted, although the sentence was sent back more than once for revisal. However, before he was liberated, he was forced to pay an immense fine. And his wife and children were detained as hostages for his banishing himself to Panama, or some place not nearer.

He took refuge on board the *Alacrity*, and then went into the *Doris*, where he won the esteem and regard of every person on board both ships. San Martin has vulgarly been said to drink: I believe this is not true; but he is an opium eater,* and his starts of passion are so frequent and violent, that no man feels his head safe. . . .

July 2d

To-day, as I was standing on the hill behind my house admiring the beautiful landscape before me, and the shadows over the sea as the clouds rolled swiftly along, and sometimes concealed and sometimes displayed the cliffs of Valparaiso, the scene was rendered more grand by the firing a salute from the *Aurora*, the smoke from which, after creeping in fleecy whiteness along the water, gradually dilated into volumes of grey cloud, and mixed with the vapours that lay on the bosoms of the hills.

This salute was in honour of Lord Cochrane, who had gone on board that frigate on his return from Santiago. His Lordship rode down to my house in the evening to tea. He tells me he has leave of absence for four months, with the schooner *Montezuma* at his disposal, and that he means to go to visit the estate in Conception decreed to him by the government long ago, but from which he has, as yet, derived no advantage, although it is one of the most fertile of that fertile province. . . .

July 7th

Yesterday morning I rode early to the port, on Lord Cochrane's invitation, to join a party which was to sail with him in the steam-vessel, the *Rising Star*, to his estate of Quintero, which lies due north from this place about twenty miles, though the road by land, being round the bay of Concon, is thirty.

Our company consisted of Don Jose Zenteno, governor of Valparaiso, his daughter Señora donna Dolores, the honourable

---

* In fact San Martin took opium as a pain-killer.

Captain Frederick Spencer, of His Majesty's ship *Alacrity*, Captain Crosbie, Captain Wilkinson, some other officers of the Patriot squadron* with whom I am not acquainted, besides some other gentlemen.

The admiral went on board with me about ten o'clock. The first thing I did was to visit the machinery, which consists of two steam-engines, each of forty-five horse power, and the wheels covered so as not to show in the water from without. The vessel is a fine polacre,† and was in great forwardness before Lord Cochrane came here, but only arrived in these seas this year.

It was with no small delight that I set my foot on the deck of the first steam-vessel that ever navigated the Pacific, and I thought, with exultation, of the triumphs of man over the obstacles nature seems to have placed between him and the accomplishment of his imaginations. . . .

I trust the time is not far distant, when the *Rising Star* will not be the only steam-vessel on the coast, and that the wise and benevolent views with which she was brought out will be fulfilled. . . .

I had as much conversation with Zenteno as my yet imperfect knowledge of Spanish would permit. He seems truly desirous of the good of Chile, but wonderfully unknowing in those things which would most contribute to it.

The morning, however, passed pleasantly away, and we sat down to a table which Europe and America equally supplied with luxuries, and amused ourselves, perhaps unseasonably, with the gluttony of the curate of Placilia, . . .

The poor curate, who had on various occasions been treated with English beer by his foreign friends, now took Champagne for *white beer*, and drank it accordingly, vowing he would grant absolution unconditionally for a hundred years, to all who drank of such divine liquor, and would doubtless have made a second Caliban of himself, and worshipped the bottle-bearer, but for an accident that rendered us all a little grave.

A small bolt in the machinery gave way, principally from imperfect fitting, as this was the first time the machinery had been fairly tried in these seas, and our voyage was stopped just as we were nearly abreast of Quintero. The wind was ahead, but we were so near that it was voted almost by acclamation that we should go on, and accordingly we trusted to the tide to take us into port. . . .

* Commanded by Lord Cochrane.
† A three-masted vessel with fore and main masts each in one piece.

The evening closed in, and it was a dull, raw, foggy night. Those not accustomed to the sea grew faint and weary. The curate, and other partakers of the *white beer*, began to feel its effects, combined with those of the motion of the vessel, now considerably agitated by the waves, which began to rise obedient to a very fresh contrary wind which had sprung up. All agreed to retire to rest.

Shortly after the strangers were in bed, the sails which had not been bent* (so sure had we been of making our passage), were got to the yards, and the first thing that happened was, that the two chimneys belonging to the engines went through the foresail. Then the wind and weather increased, and the furniture began to roll about, and at last, in the morning, we found ourselves farther than ever from our place of destination.

However, breakfast gave us courage, and it was determined to persevere a few hours longer. But the weather grew worse and worse, the sky became blacker and blacker, so at length we bore up for Valparaiso, and landed there at two o'clock to-day.

A great pleasure awaited us, and almost consoled us for the failure of our expedition. That is, if ever public news consoles one for private disappointment. Mr Hogan met me on the beach with the joyful intelligence that the Congress of the United States had acknowledged the independence of the Spanish American colonies of Mexico, Columbia, Buenos Ayres, Peru, and Chile.

This is indeed a step gained, and so naturally too, as to be worth twenty, where there could have been a suspicion of intrigue. But the United States, themselves so lately emancipated from the thraldom of the mother-country, are the natural assertors of the independence of their American brethren, and the moral of the political history of the times would have been less striking had any other state set the example. . . .

July 8th

To-day, a young man born in Cundinamarca, but brought up in Quito, came to stay to me, that I may put him in the way of improving a great natural talent for drawing. He has been long on board Lord Cochrane's ship, in I know not what capacity, and has displayed considerable taste in some sketches of costume, &c.

The people of Quito pride themselves on retaining that excellence of painting which distinguished their predecessors of the time of Pizarro. Of course the Christian priests have introduced

* Fastened.

European models and European practice, but the talent for the imitative arts is said to be inherent in all, or almost all the Quiteños, and it is certain that the painters, whether of portraits or history, that are to be met with in various parts of South America, are almost universally Quiteños.

My scholar is gentle and persevering, rather indolent, possessed of good sense, and a strong poetical feeling.

If I had him in Europe, where he could see good pictures, and above all, good drawings, I have no doubt but he would be a painter. As it is, seeing nothing much better than his own, there is little chance of very great improvement. . . .

July 10th

Capt.—— breakfasted with me, and afterwards was so kind as to accompany me in a round of calls, by way of returning the visits of the English ladies here.

It is curious, at this distance from home, to see specimens of such people as one meets nowhere else but among the Brangtons, in Madame D'Arblay's *Cecilia*, or the Mrs Eltons of Miss Austen's admirable novels, and yet these are, after all, the people most likely to be here.

The country is new, the government unacknowledged by our own, the merchants are chiefly such as sell by commission, for houses established in larger and older states. And, as all Englishmen, from the highest to the lowest, love to have their *home* with them, the clerks, who fall naturally into these sort of employments, either bring or find suitable wives, therefore society, as far as relates to the English, is of a very low tone. . . .

16th

We have had two slight shocks of an earthquake to-day. The sensations occasioned by them are particularly disagreeable. In all other convulsions of nature it seems possible to do, or at least attempt, something to avert danger.

We steer the ship in a storm for a port, our conductors promise to lead the lightning harmless from our heads, but the earthquake seems to rock the very foundations of the globe, and escape or shelter seems equally impossible. The physical effect too is unpleasant – it resembles sea-sickness. . . . One of the shocks to-day lasted nearly a minute, it was accompanied by a loud noise, like the sudden escape of vapour from a close place. . . .

18th

The earthquakes have been followed by two days of incessant rain, but the thermometer, though it is mid-winter, has not fallen below 50°.

The rivulet between the Almendral and my garden is so swollen, that there has been no communication with the town these two days, and a man was drowned yesterday in attempting to cross it.

There is a report that this government will join the Peruvian in an attack on Arica, where the royalists are again masters, and that the Admiral* is to conduct the expedition.

'Tis not probable. In the first place, His Lordship has returned to his country seat, having leave of absence for four months, and in the next, the ships of the Chileno squadron are in no state to go to sea. And as the officers and seamen have not been paid, it is scarcely possible for the government to think of employing them.

22d

The wet weather continues, though with hours of sunshine occasionally. I have been delighted with reading the first new books I have seen in Chile, Lord Byron's *Foscari*, *Cain*, and *Sardanapalus*. He cannot write without stirring our feelings. . . .

The reading of these dramas has afforded me great enjoyment – and 'tis the first for many a day. . . .

July 30th

As there are no places of public amusement for gentlefolks at Valparaiso, the English, when they make a holyday, go in parties to the neighbouring hills or valleys, and under the name of a pic-nic, contrive to ride, eat and drink, and even to dance away most gaily.

I joined one of the soberer kind of these, and rode over a good deal of ground with my younger friends, sometimes over steep rocks, sometimes through dingles and bushy dells, and here and there through bits of meadow, where the finest mushrooms in the world grow. The peach and cherry trees are in blossom, and all looks gay and cheerful.

Most of us went to the place of rendezvous in the valley of Palms on horseback, but some preferred the quieter conveyance of a

---

* Lord Cochrane.

Chile waggon, drawn by four noble oxen, who had to drag the additional weight of an excellent dinner.

The spot was at the foot of a steep hill covered with myrtle. Our canopy, hung something like the draperies that Claude sometimes introduces in his landscapes, was the striped and starred banner of the United States, whose consul was the father of the feast, and close by us flowed a rivulet of sparkling water. The kind-hearted Chilena women of the neighbouring rancho came round us, assisted in our little arrangements, brought us flowers, and helped us to cut the myrtle of which we made our seats.

Some were very happy, but happiness is not of everyday growth, and there are not many hands destined to pluck the golden bough. But it is always worth while to be cheerful, and I enjoyed the day more than I thought three months ago I could have enjoyed any thing. . . .

She was beginning to recover, to turn outward.

On 12 August, with Don, her old pointer following, she rode out after breakfast to her friends, the Miers, fifteen miles away at Concon.

John Miers had come to Chile in 1818 with a project for setting up copper mills in the country, where copper was half and labour a quarter the cost in England, and coal 'dirt cheap'. In the event the one hundred and seventy tons of machinery he brought with him in ships for the purpose had to be adapted instead to flour milling since, as Maria Graham commented, it 'was a hundred years too civilized for Chile', where men were still digging their gardens with the blade bone of a sheep tied to a stick in lieu of spades.

After a pleasant day with the Miers, 'seeing things fit and unfit for the present state of things in the country',[1] Maria and her friends set out the following day to visit Lord Cochrane's estate, not far off, at Quintero, where he was building a house.

'But who could think of the house when the master is present?' mused Maria, for although the admiral could not be considered handsome, there was an expression on his face 'which induces you when you have looked once, to look again and again'.[2]

She enjoyed everything. The admiral's conversation (when on the rare occasion he broke his customary silence); his plans for introducing modern farming methods to the estate, and, later that evening, when she looked over with him the various designs for the small trading vessels he intended to employ along the Chilean coast.

The next morning she saw a rodeo, spent the early afternoon planting strawberries and fruit trees in the admiral's garden, and later left with the Miers determined, after such a successful expedition, to make a journey to see Chile's capital, Santiago.

Santiago was ninety miles away, a three-day ride. Arrangements were at once put in hand. Three mules to carry the baggage, a peon as guide, her personal maid as attendant, and Frederick de Roos, a midshipman from HMS **Alacrity**, as riding companion.

They set out on August 22, riding through a landscape that reminded them both of Devonshire. Then, just before Casablanca, it changed, and they found themselves moving through a plain of heavily scented mimosa, the earth at their feet carpeted, she noted, with thrift, wood anemones and Star of Bethlehem.

By this time her maid was so 'fagged' that Maria was beginning to wish she'd never brought her. However, they halted at an inn kept by an English black 'who understands something of the comfort required by an Englishman',[3] and next day rode on through country that this time put her in mind of the Apennines.

They stopped for the night at a post house kept by an old woman who provided very good mutton and excellent claret, and gave them a clean room to sleep in. Maria's maid, 'fagged' again, retired early, while Maria stayed up to write her journal and get things ready for the following day, dryly remarking that 'youth and health are not always the hardiest travelling companions'.[4]

At seven next morning they were off, their road taking them over the mountain, Cuesta de Prado, at the summit of which they reined in, and, through 'the leafy gulf at their feet', saw the plain of Santiago, and, far off, the city, with its spires dazzling white in the morning sun.

They slowly descended, and at the foot of the mountain breakfasted on boiled mutton, after which (poor maid!) they rode on, when, outside the next post house, they were met by Don Jose Antonio de Cotapos with an invitation for Maria to stay with him and his family in Santiago.

They were joined not long after by two carriages containing Madame de Cotapos and her three lovely daughters, all equally pressing. So it was that Maria, who had secretly intended to stay at an English inn in the city in order to be free to do as she liked, was conducted in triumph to the Casa Cotapos.

25 August – 7 September 1822

25th August

The house of Cotapos is handsomely, not elegantly, furnished. Good mirrors, handsome carpets, a piano by Broadwood, and a reasonable collection of chairs, tables, and beds, not just of the forms of modern Paris or London, but such, I dare say, as were fashionable there little more than a century ago, look exceedingly well on this side of the Horn.

It is only the dining-room that I feel disposed to quarrel with. It is the darkest, dullest, and meanest apartment in the house. The table is stuck in one corner, so that one end and one side only allow room for a row of high chairs between them and the wall, therefore any thing like the regular attendance of servants is precluded. One would almost think that it was arranged for the purpose of eating in secret. And one is led to think, especially when the great gates close at night before the principal meal is presented, of the Moors and the Israelites of the Spanish peninsula, jealously hiding themselves from the eyes of their Gothic tyrants.

My breakfast was served in my own room according to my own fashion, with tea, eggs, and bread and butter. The family eat nothing at this time of day, but some take a cup of chocolate, others a little broth, and most a matee. The ladies all visited me on their way to mass, and on this occasion they had left off their usual French style of dress, and were in black, with the Mantilla and all that makes a pretty Spaniard or Chilena, ten times prettier.

About noon, M. de la Salle, one of the Supreme Director's Aides de Camp called, with a polite compliment from His Excellency,* welcoming me to Santiago. By this gentleman I sent my letters of introduction to Doña Rosa O'Higgins; and it was agreed that I should visit her to-morrow evening, as she goes to the theatre to-night. . . .

26th

This morning, on looking out soon after day-break, I saw the provisions coming into town for the market. The beef cut in

* Dom Bernardo O'Higgins.

quarters, the mutton in halves, was mounted on horseback before a man or boy, who, in his poncho, sat as near the tail of the horse as possible. Fowls in large grated chests of hide came slung on mules. Eggs, butter, milk, cheese, and vegetables, all rode, no Chileno condescending to walk, especially with a burden, unless in case of dire necessity. And as the strings of beasts so laden came along one way, I saw women enveloped in their mantos, and carrying their alfombras and missals, going to Mass another.

The cries in the streets are nearly as unintelligible as those in London, and, with the exception of *Sweep* and *Old Clothes*, concern the same articles.

Judge Prevost came in soon after breakfast and settled my mode of paying my respects to Doña Rosa O'Higgins in the evening. It appears that to walk even to a next-door neighbour on occasions of ceremony is so undignified, that I must not think of it, therefore I go in a chaise belonging to the family where I live, and two of the ladies will accompany me.

This last proposal I own startled me. They are of one of the best families here, but a daughter was married to a Carrera.*

They were all partizans of Carrera, and more than one have been implicated in conspiracies against the present government, nay, it is said against the Director's life. And I know that no intercourse of a friendly nature, notwithstanding the good-natured wishes of Mr Prevost, has as yet taken place between the palace and the house of Cotapos.

If I am the means of spreading peace, so much the better, though I perhaps would rather know openly the use to be made of me. . . .

We came home to dress for the palace, where we went accompanied by Judge Prevost, Madame Cotapos and her second daughter, Mariquita, a young woman more cultivated than is usual here.

The ladies both apologized for appearing in cotton stockings and coarse black shoes, by saying that it was in consequence of a vow made during a severe illness of the old gentleman, Don José Miguel Cotapos, by which they had obliged themselves to wear such stockings and shoes a whole year, if his life was granted to their prayers.

If I smiled at the superstition of this, the affection whence it proceeded was too respectable to permit me to laugh, and I was well aware of the extent of the merit of the vow, as there is nothing in which a lady of Chile is so delicate as the choice of her shoes.

* José Miguel Carrera had been the arch-rival of O'Higgins in the early fight for Chilean independence.

Madame Cotapos whispered to me that the torment hers had occasioned was such that she had been obliged to slip a little cotton wool into them to save her feet. . . .

On arriving at the palace, we walked in with less bustle and attendance than I have seen in most private houses. The rooms were handsomely but plainly furnished, English cast-iron grates, Scotch carpets, some French china, and timepieces, little or nothing that looked Spanish, still less Chileno.

The Director's mother Doña Isabella, and his sister Doña Rosa, received us not only politely but kindly. The Director's reception was exceedingly flattering both to me and my young friend De Roos. His Excellency had passed several years in England, a great part of which time he spent at an academy at Richmond in Surrey.

He immediately asked me if I had ever been there, enquired after my uncle Mr, now Sir, David Dundas,* and several other persons of my acquaintance, by name, and asked very particularly about his old masters in music and other arts. I was very much pleased with the kindliness of nature shown in these recollections, and still more so when I saw several wild-looking little girls come into the room, and run up to him, and cling about his knees, and found they were little orphan Indians rescued from slaughter on the field of battle.

It appears that the Indians, when they make their inroads on the reclaimed grounds, bring their wives and families with them, and should a battle take place and become desperate, the women usually take part in it. Should they lose it, it is not uncommon for the men to put to death their wives and children to prevent them from falling into the hands of the enemy, and indeed till now it was only anticipating, by a few minutes, the fate of these wretched creatures. For quarter was neither given nor taken on either side, the Indians in the Spanish ranks continuing their own war customs in spite of their partial civilization. The Director now gives a reward for all persons, especially women and children, saved on these occasions.

The children are to be educated and employed hereafter as mediators between their nations and Chile, and, to this end, care is taken that they should not forget their native tongue. The Director was kind enough to talk to them in the Araucanian tongue, that I might hear the language, which is soft and sweet; perhaps it owed something to the young voices of the children. . . . Doña Rosa

* General Sir David Dundas (1735–1820). Reorganized the British Army along the lines of the Prussian Army.

takes a particular charge of the little female prisoners, and acts the part of a kind mother to them. I was charmed with the humane and generous manner in which she spoke of them.

As to Doña Isabella, she appears to live on her son's fame and greatness, and looks at him with the eyes of maternal love, and gathers every compliment to him with eagerness.

He is modest and simple, and plain in his manners, arrogating nothing to himself, or if he has done much, ascribing it to the influence of that love of country which, as he says, may inspire great feelings into an ordinary man.

He conversed very freely about the state of Chile, and told me he doubted not but that I must be surprised at the backwardness of the country in many things, and particularly mentioned the want of religious toleration, or, rather, the very small measure of it which, considering the general state of things, he had yet been able to grant, without disturbing the public tranquillity. He seemed a little inclined to censure those Protestants who wished prematurely to force upon him the building a chapel, and the public institution of Protestant worship, forgetting how very short a time it is since even private liberty of conscience and a consecrated burial-place had been allowed in a country which, within twelve years, had been subject to the Inquisition at Lima.

He spoke a good deal also of the necessity of public education, and told me of the Lancasterian and other schools lately established here, and in other towns in Chile, which are certainly numerous in proportion to the population. . . .

The Director was dressed, as I believe he always is, in his general's uniform. He is short and fat, yet very active, his blue eyes, light hair, and ruddy and rather coarse complexion, do not bely his Irish extraction, while his very small and short hands and feet belong to his Araucanian pedigree.

Doña Isabella is young-looking for her years, and very handsome, though small. Her daughter is like the Director, on a larger scale. She was dressed in a scarlet satin spencer and white skirt, a sort of dress much worn here. The Chileno men are an uglier coarser race, as far as I have seen, than the women, who are beautiful, and, what is more, lady-like. They have a natural easy politeness, and a caressing manner that is delightful, but then some of their habits are disagreeable.

For instance, a handsome fat lady, who came all in blue satin to the palace to-night, had a spitting-box brought and set before her, into which she spat continually, and so dexterously, as to show she was well accustomed to the manoeuvre. However, the young ladies, and all who would be thought so, are leaving off these ugly habits fast.

At about ten o'clock we left the palace, and found our young people at home still engaged in their minuets. I sat with them a short time, and then came to my alto to write the journal of this my second day in Santiago, with which I am very well pleased. . . .

28th – St Austin's Day

I am no favourite with the saint, for he has been thwarting me all day long. But all things in order.

Early in the morning I heard a bell ringing exactly like that which on winter evenings in London announces the approach of 'muffins'.

I looked out, and saw first, a boy ringing the said bell, then another with a bundle of candles, all the people in the street pulled off their hats, and stood as if doing homage.

Then came a dark blue caleche, with glories and holy ghosts painted on it, and a man within dressed in white satin, embroidered with silver and coloured silk. In front sat a man with a gilt lanthorn, behind people with umbrellas.

I asked what it was, and was told it was the *Padre Eterno*. The expression sounds indecent to a protestant, it is holy to a Spaniard, who must think that such indeed is the Host on its way to a dying person – such in fact was the procession I saw.

This was the only thing that happened before the disappointments occasioned by St Austin began. The first of these occurred when I went with Mr de Roos to see the Lancasterian school. We found the boys all gone to Mass in honour of St Austin, and the school shut. We proceeded to the national printing-office. The doors were shut, and the printers at Mass.

Thence we went to the chamber of the Consulada, hoping to be present at a session of the convention. But the members were at Mass. Then despairing of seeing any public place or people, I thought I would draw, so repaired to the Plaça, where I had been promised a balcony to sketch from. But the master had gone to Mass, and taken the keys in his pocket, so I went home, resolving to do better in the afternoon, and began to sketch the inner pateo of the house. But, being a holiday, numerous visitors came, and little was done. . . .

There now began a series of extensive outings with Mr de Roos as ever-agreeable companion.

An expedition to the Sala Agua or Water Leap, where could be seen the magnificent irrigation works of the ancient Cacique Indians, and where Maria gazed dreamily at the cascade 'in the spirit of Ossian'. As she did so she experienced the curious feeling that the soul of some old Cacique had flitted by, gratified not only by the fruitfully smiling plains with which his work had been rewarded, but by her own presence, 'as one of the white children of the East, whence freedom to the sons of the Indians was once more to arise'.[1]

In this agreeable state of mind she returned to Santiago to find a troop of servants in full livery delivering trays covered by embroidered napkins on which were arranged melons, oranges and sweet limes as well as the rarest and most beautiful flowers. They were a present from Doña Rosa, the Director's wife.

Next evening she attended the theatre for the first time. King Ninus the Second *was showing, a play she'd never heard of, though discovered it was a tale of 'love and murder'. Her mind may still have been running on agreeable sensations of grandeur, for when the Director came into the theatre she found herself absently rising and curtseying as she would naturally have done in the presence of royalty, only to become aware she was the only person in the house to have done so. Her chagrin, however, was much tempered by receiving an appreciative bow from the Directorial box.*

The city of Santiago was next thoroughly explored, the Mint investigated, only to reveal defective stamping machinery, irrelevantly cumbersome; the Consulado, or representative Assembly, was next attended by special permission, since she was a woman.

Here, as she and Mr de Roos sat listening, she found herself impressed by the freedom of debate, and more especially since the Assembly had been appointed, not democratically, but by the Director alone. Yet throughout the proceedings she recognized that the thinking was still of a markedly Spanish cast, something only time and education could rectify so as to produce an individually Chileno *character.*

The observation extended to the holding of land, where the grants awarded to the original Spanish settlers remained still unrevoked, causing poverty among the native Chilenos and an inadequate population rate. Nevertheless the government were currently considering inducements to encourage the Spaniards to sell land for the Indians to cultivate, while in the first year of the revolution all duty-work and slavery among them had been abolished. Maria, nevertheless had observed that considerable duty-work was still being done by peons and Indians on the estates she had visited.

'Perhaps the world never experienced so great a change as in the last thirty-five years,' she wrote, adding, 'that all should have been for the

107

*better, no one who reflects on the imperfect state of humanity, will believe;
but I will hope that most of these changes have bettered the general
condition of human nature.*[2]

Thursday, Sept. 5th

A large party, consisting of the whole of the Cotapos family, and a
number of others, amounting to thirty, including Mr Prevost, Mr
De Roos, and myself, spent a day in the country. The ladies who
did not ride went in *carretons*, small covered vehicles of the
country, in which they sit on carpets and cushions. The servants
and provisions were in another, thatched at the top exactly like a
cottage. The whole party was collected in the pateo of the Casa
Cotapos, and set off by nine o'clock, as gay as youth, health, and a
resolution to be pleased, could make them. I should say *us*; for, at
least in the resolution to be pleased, I equalled the rest.

After a short pleasant ride of about five miles to the eastward, we
reached Nnuñoa, a pleasant village, where the bishop has a seat,
and where, a chacra having been lent us for the purpose, we spent
a most agreeable day. . . .

Doña Mariquita and I, with two or three others, among whom
was Doña Mariquita's father, Don José Miguel de Cotapos, a most
gentlemanlike old man, in his poncho of plain Vicunha wool of the
natural colour, and his broad hat, his silver-mounted bridle,
stirrups, &c., rode off to a casita about two leagues farther on. . . .

On our return to the Nnuñoa we found our friends busy dancing
to the quita. They had procured two musicians to hire, and were
engaged in minuets, and Spanish country-dances, perhaps the
most graceful in the world. But what most delighted me were the
cuando and samba, danced and sung with more spirit than the city
manners allow, yet still decorous.

Dancing can express only two passions – the hatred of war, and
love. Even the grave minuet de la cour will, by its approaching,
retiring, presenting of hands, separating, and final meeting,
express the latter. How much more the rustic dance that gives the
quarrel and reconciliation! This it is which makes dancing a fine art.

The mere figures of dances where more than two are concerned,
such as vulgar French or English dances, have as little to do with
the poetry of dancing as the inventors of patterns for printed linens
have to do with the poetry of painting. My Chilenos feel dancing;
and even when they dance a Scotch reel, they contrive to infuse a
little of the spirit of the muse into it. . . .

In the evening I undertook to make tea for the dancers, after which we rode back to the city as gay a cavalcade as ever entered it, and the day was ended by a tertulla at the Casa Cotapos.

6th September

Visited several persons, English and Chileno. I say nothing of the English here, because I do not know them except as very civil vulgar people, with one or two exceptions.

Mr B., for instance, commonly called Don Diego, he has lived many years here since the revolution, and says he has never met with injustice or unkindness in the country. He knows it better than most persons.

Mr C. has gone through much – has I may say been a party in the southern war, lending his money, horses, and ships to the patriot cause, and he, I think, seems to possess the clearest ideas concerning the state of Chile of any man I have met with. And there are several very good people, some acting the fine gentleman, others playing the knave, just as it happens in other places, only I do wish that some more of the better specimens of English were here, for the honour of our nation and the benefit of Chile.

7th

I went early to the national printing-office, which is creditable enough to the little state; but the types are very scanty. I doubt if they could print a quarto of four hundred pages.

I bought the gazettes from 1818 to the present time, nothing was printed here before. I also got some laws, rules, and songs. Under the old Spanish government I believe Chile had no press at all, but am not quite sure, nor could I learn. But every thing necessary was printed at Lima, i.e. every thing that the Viceroy, the Archbishop, and the Grand Inquisitor chose to promulgate.

In the afternoon we went to visit the nuns of St Augustin's. Thank God, by the new regulations the convents have all become so poor, that there is good hope the number will soon diminish.

These nuns are old and ugly, with the exception of one, who is young, has sweet eyes, and is very pale, a dangerous beauty for a cavalier. She moved my pity.

The old ladies gave us matee, the best I have tasted, made with milk and Chile cinnamon, and the cup was set in a tray of flowers, so that both taste and smell were gratified. This convent is one of the finest in Chile, having seven quadrangles. We saw through the parlour into one of them, where, in the centre of a pool, there is the ugliest Virgin that man ever cut in stone, intended to spout water from her mouth and breast. But she is now idle, as the fountain is under repair, and the masons, with half a dozen soldiers to guard them or the nuns, were busy round the pool.

During the short time I remained at the grate, I heard more gossip than I have done for months, and perceived that the recluses continue to take a lively interest in the things of this wicked world. I was not sorry when summoned to go to another place, and having left a golden remembrancer with the good ladies, I accompanied Mr Prevost and Mr de Roos to the public library. . . .

8 September – 24 September 1822

September 8th

I bought my roan horse Fritz. He has white feet, and two blue eyes, is tall and strong, and never carried a woman in his life. But I wanted to give my pet *Charles* some rest, so thought twenty dollars not too much. Therefore I gave it at once, mounted Fritz without ceremony, and rode to the Director's chacra with Mr de Roos, to pay a forenoon visit. We were not allowed, however, to leave it before dinner. We found the ladies sitting in their garden, with their little Indian girls playing about them. . . .

Fortunately for us there were no strangers but ourselves, and the Director readily led the conversation to the affairs of Chile, and to the events of his own life.

Of the recent affairs in Peru (the displacing Monteagudo,* &c.) he expressed himself with regret, considering that minister's conduct, and the consequences of it, as a stain on the good cause. I wish I had dared to hint, that a conduct as bad, though in a different way, in Rodriguez, his own minister, was producing effects at least as vexatious here.

We walked a good deal about the gardens, and amused ourselves for some time with a fine telescope, through which the Director pointed out to me many farms on the plain of Maypu, in the line of the canal of irrigation which he has made since he was Director, where all was formerly barren, and behind whose thickets robbers and murderers concealed themselves, so that the roads were unsafe. These ruffians have now disappeared, and peaceful farms occupy the ground.

From the garden we went in to dinner, where all was plain and handsome. English neatness gave the Chileno dishes every thing I had ever thought wanting in them. Doña Isabella, Doña Rosa, Doña Xaviera the Director's niece a beautiful young woman, and one aide-de-camp, besides ourselves, formed the whole party.

The little Indians had a low table in the corner, where the little daughter of the Cacique† presided, and where they were served with as much respect as Doña Rosa herself.

* General San Martin's unpopular right-hand man.
† Political boss, i.e. the Director.

111

The entrance of some strangers after dinner put an end to all confidential intercourse, and I then walked about the house with Doña Isabella. The ladies' bed-rooms are neat and comfortable in every way. The Director, when here, sleeps on a little portable camp-bed, and to judge by his room, is not very studious of personal accommodation.

At sunset we returned to town, and at the same time His Excellency's family went thither also to attend the opera, which Doña Rosa never misses. Their equipage is English, and though plain, handsome. . . .

Another expedition had already been planned. This time a nine-hour ride over the Maypu plain to visit the ranch of the eldest married Cotapos daughter, Ana Maria.

There were four in the party with Maria: a Cotapos son and Don José Antonio and his sister, Doña Rosario, besides the irreplaceable Mr de Roos. Maria's unsatisfactory maid appears not to have been of the party.

The Cotapos daughter, it transpired, had been married to one of the famous Carrera brothers, an interesting circumstance, which appears to have inspired a surge of romanticism in Maria. On their arrival at the hacienda she stood entranced as her hostess approached, 'She has one of the most beautiful faces I ever beheld:' she wrote 'an eye both to entreat and command; and a mouth which neither painter or sculptor, in his imagined Hebes or Graces, could equal.'[1]

Four nights were to be spent at the hacienda, which was extremely comfortable, the hostess thoughtfully providing Maria and Mr de Roos with an English breakfast of eggs and bread and butter, rather than the more robust Chilean version of soup, meat and wine.

Maria, as was her custom, rose early. A useful habit she tells us since 'it anticipated intrusion, the privacy of bedrooms is not respected in Chile as in England'.[2]

She spent her time inspecting the estate; noted the roots of the vines were not trimmed annually as in Italy, but only once every twenty or thirty years; visited the dairy, which in her opinion was being wastefully conducted; saw a curious sheep with five horns; tasted the local wine, very pleasant, the brandy especially good.

That evening she sketched while a guest played the guitar and sang gaucho songs. These Maria later wrote down, though to her mind the words were about as significant as 'Hey diddle diddle'.

Next day they rode out over fallen aromatic leaves to Lake Aculeo, which reminded her of the Lago Maggiore. She tasted the water, made a sketch, and afterwards they rode home in the twilight to be met at the door by her host with two guests, one of them peculiarly arresting by reason of his extraordinary beauty. Unfortunately, Maria was told, he was a tonto *– mentally deficient.*

'*It made me quite melancholy,*'[3] *she wrote, and when she eventually went to bed was unable to sleep for thinking of him.*

Due perhaps to the young man's presence, a melancholy seems to have overcome the house party. They spent the last day with a picnic overlooking a ravishing view, drinking maté out of silver cups, and listening to the tragic story of their hostess, Doña Ana. Convents, intrigues, imprisonment, secret cyphers, love and death – by the time Maria returned to the hacienda she was in a mood to respond to a drama that seemed straight out of her favourite Byron's Manfred.

She settled down to draw. As before, the tonto *was present, only this time Maria thought she noticed an occasional flash of intelligence brighten his eye. Convinced by now that he was in some way a tragic victim of the civil war, she casually mentioned that the Director had promised to consider an amnesty for anyone caught up in the politics of the revolution.*

'*There was something in the faces of all that induced me to repeat this distinctly again,*' *she records. At this moment she observed the* tonto *whispering something to Doña Ana.*

'*And why should not you, who live in the country and have your farm, be happy as all of us?*' *she asked him boldly.*

'*I happy with farms and peons, and cattle! No!*' *he cried,* '*for years I was wretched, and the first moment of happiness I owe to you!*'

'*Indeed! then you are not what you seem?*' *asked Maria.*

At this the erstwhile tonto *rose, his eye flashing fire.*

'*No, – I will no longer play this fool's part; it is unworthy the son of Xabiera, the nephew of José Miguel Carrera!*' *the* tonto *cried passionately.* '*I am that unhappy exile Lastra, reduced to fly from desert to desert, to hide me in caves, and to feed with the fowls of the air, till my limbs are palsied and my youth is wasted; and my crime has been to love Chile. Oh, my country! What would I not suffer for thee!*'[4]

Maria who for whatever reason had self-confessedly remained immoveable throughout this outburst now rose.

'. . . *I gave him my hand, and desired he would come to see me in Santiago, like himself [presumably in his right mind] after the 18th.* '*This,*' *commented Maria complacently,* '*restored us to our ordinary state of cheerfulness.*'[5]

The morning of the 13th (marked 11th in the journal, owing perhaps to anxiety), Doña Rosario, her brother, Mr de Roos and Maria set off for Melipilla.

Their send-off was suitably eerie, and in accordance with the events of the previous evening. Dense fog shut out the mountains, and it was drizzling. By the time they drew rein at the famous estate of the Marques la

113

Rayna, however, the sky was clearing, and Maria had regained her sang froid.

Having been shown round the estate with all its offices, including the slaughterhouses, she mused for much of the remainder of the eighty-mile ride on how wasteful the butchery arrangements of Chile were – heads, bones, hearts, livers, all profligately thrown away, likewise horns, hoofs and, again, bones utterly wasted. . . .

They reached Melipilla as night was falling, found a good house (roast beef, stewed fowl, good bread, and a bottle of very tolerable wine) and soon retired.

'The beds appeared to embarrass Mr de Roos more than anything,' wrote Maria, 'but I am an old traveller, and our Chileno friends are used to this sort of thing; so my young Englishman made up his mind to our all passing the night within the same four walls.'⁶

As a concession to Mr de Roos's sensibility however she spread the long skirt of her riding habit over a line of high-backed chairs, thus separating the ladies from the gentlemen, after which they slept soundly till morning.

15th September

This morning Doña Rosario and her brother went to early Mass, while Mr de Roos and I prepared all things for beginning our journey back to Santiago. . . . We had no intention this day of going farther than San Francisco de Monte, where there is a tolerable house for travellers, kept by an old servant of a relation of the Cotapos.

As soon as we arrived there, the gentlemen rode off to visit a relation of our companions, while Doña Rosario and I remained to perform rather a more careful toilette than we had been able to do at Melipilla.

The house we were in is, in all senses, a pulperia, combining the characters of a huckster's shop and an alehouse. The host has some Indian and some African blood in his veins, and is a shrewd ingenious man. He has set up a proper loom for weaving ponchos, by which means he produces more work in a week than the weavers of Melipilla in a month. His wife spins and dyes the wool, and by this trade, and the profits of their shop, they earn a very decent livelihood.

As soon as I had changed my dress I went out to walk round the little town, which I found laid out with great neatness, and admired the gardens and fields, though I could perceive that San Francisco had once boasted inhabitants of a higher class than those I saw. The best houses are shut up, and there was an air of decay in their immediate neighbourhood. They did belong to the Carreras. The heiress, Doña Xaviera, is now living as an exile at Monte Video.

I went towards the Plaça, where there are the church and convent of the Franciscans, and several extremely good houses. I was attracted by a great crowd at the door of one of these. The mounted guasos were standing by with their hats off, and every body seemed as if performing an act of devotion. I was a little astonished when I arrived at the centre of the crowd, to which every body made way for me, to find nine persons dancing, as the Spaniards say, *con mucho compas*.

They were arranged like nine-pins, the centre one being a young boy dressed in a grotesque manner, who only changed his place occasionally with two others, one of whom had a guitar, the other a ravel. The height and size of limb of the dancers might have belonged to men, the apparel was female, and I thought I had been suddenly introduced to a tribe of Patagonian women, and enquired of a bystander whence they came, when I received the following information concerning the dancers and the dance.

When the Franciscans first began the conversion of the Indians in this part of Chile, they fixed their convent at Talagante, the village of the palms which we passed through the other day, their proselytes being the caciques of Talagante, Yupeo, and Chenigue. The good fathers found that the Indians were more easily brought over to a new faith, than weaned from certain superstitious practices belonging to their old idolatry, and the annual dance under the shade of the cinnamon, in honour of a preserving Power, they found it impossible to make them forget. They therefore permitted them to continue it, but it was to be performed within the convent walls, and in honour of Nuestra Señora de la Merced, and each cacique in turn was to take upon him the expense of the feast.

On the removal of the convent to its present station the dance was allowed in the church, and the dancers, instead of painted bodies, and heads crowned with feathers, and bound with the fillet (still thought holy), are now clothed completely in women's dresses, as fine as they can procure. And as the priests have much abridged the period of the solemnity, they are fain to finish their dance in the area before the church, where they are attended with as much deference as in the temple itself. After having performed this duty, the dancers, and as many as choose to accompany them, repair to the Cacique's house, where they are treated with all the food he can command, and drink till his stock of chicha is exhausted.

I considered myself very fortunate in having met with these dancers, and pleased myself with the idea that they were the descendants of the Promaucians, who had resisted the Incas in their endeavours to subdue the country, and who, after bravely disputing its possession with the Spaniards, being once induced to make a league with them never deserted them.

I was lucky too in the person to whom I applied for information. He is a deformed, but sprightly-looking man, who acts the double part of schoolmaster and *gracioso* of the village. While we sat at dinner to-day he entered to pay his compliments, and began a long extempore compliment to each of us in verse, in a manner at least as good as that of the common *improvisatori* of Italy.

For this I paid him with a cup of wine, when he began to recite the collection of legendary and other verses, till, heated I presume by the glasses handed to him by our young men, his tales began to stray so far from decorum that we silenced the old gentleman, and sent him to get a good dinner with the peons. . . .

16th Sept.

We left San Francisco by Talagante, intending to go close by the mountain of San Miguel, to the farm where the new Mapocho comes by several copious springs from under-ground.

We stopped at the Cacique's to pay our compliments, and bought some small jars and platters of red clay, ornamented with streaks of earth, to which iron pyrites give the appearance of gold dust.

Talagante is a very populous village, and the women at every hut appear to be potters. The men are soldiers, sailors, carriers, and some few husbandmen, a fine, handsome, that is, well-made race, with faces very Indian.

We had scarcely left it a league, when I was obliged to lag a little behind the party by a violent cough, and then I broke a small blood-vessel. It was some time before I could rejoin my friends, and then there was great consternation among them, as we were at least ten leagues from home.

I proposed to them to ride on, and leave me to proceed slowly with the peon. This they refused to do, and the hemorrhage increasing, I felt pleased that they remained with me. I had nothing with me to stop the bleeding, and I longed for water, on which Don José Antonio recollecting a spring not far off, he and Mr de Roos rode off to it, and filling the little jars we had brought with us, we put some orange-peel into it, and whenever the cough returned I took a mouthful.

I found I dared not speak, nor ride fast, so at a foot's pace we went on to Santiago. I had two very serious attacks before I reached the city, but, on the whole, I cannot say I suffered much. It was a delightful day, and the scenery was beautiful and grand.

We crossed the plain of Maypu farther to the westward, and nearer the scene of the great action* than before. The ground was covered with flowers, and flocks of birds were collected round them. I thought if it were to be my last ride out among the works of God, it was one to soothe and comfort me; and I did not feel at all depressed. I may think, with more ease than most, of my end, detached as I now am from all kindred.

A few miles before we reached home Mr de Roos rode on, and having told Doña Carmen what had happened, she ordered my maid to have fire, warm water, and my bed prepared. Mr de Roos also found Dr Craig, who came immediately, and as I was almost without fever and very well disposed to sleep soundly, the accident of the day promised to be of little consequence.

17th

Letters from Valparaiso announce the arrival of the *Doris*, and that my poor cousin Glennie has taken possession of my house, being in a state of health that gives little hope of his recovery.

He broke a blood-vessel in consequence of over-exertion at Callao, and is obliged to invalid, as the surgeon thinks the voyage round the Horn, whither the ship is bound, would be fatal.

It is very distressing to me not to be able to go instantly to Valparaiso to receive him, but I am confined to bed myself. I have also kind letters from Lord Cochrane, enclosing an introduction to General Freire,† in case I should ride down to Conception, as I intended, from hence, but proposing the better plan of going by sea in the *Montezuma*, when His Lordship himself goes.

Alas! I can do neither, and I fear I must give up my hopes of visiting Peru, as well as going to the south of Chile. My own slight illness I should think nothing of, but the poor invalid at Valparaiso must have all my time and attention.

* At the battle of Maypu in April 1818 San Martin defeated the Spanish royalists.
† General Freire ultimately displaced O'Higgins as Director of Chile.

18th

The anniversary of the independence of Chile.

The first thing I heard after a long sleepless night was the trampling of horses; and I got out of bed and went to the balcony, whence I saw the country militia going to the ground where the Director is to review them all.

They are in number about two thousand, armed with lances, twenty feet long, of cane, headed with iron. The men are dressed in their ordinary dress, with military caps and scarlet ponchos, and the different divisions are distinguished by borders or collars, or some other trivial mark.

I have heard many jests upon the discipline of the red cloaks, but B., who knows them well, says,

'True, they may on parade mistake *eyes right* for *eyes left*, but at the battle of Maypu they never mistook the enemy', and, in truth, on that day, when the regular troops had begun to give ground, they are said to have turned the fortune of the day.

They are admirable horsemen, as indeed every country-bred Chileno is. They ride like centaurs, seeming to make but one person with their horse, and I have seen them wrestle and fight on horseback as if they had been on foot.

I was glad the Casa Cotapos stands so directly in the way of the exercising ground. The only compensation I can have for not being present at the national rejoicing is the seeing the troops pass. . . .

I felt low and ill all day.

21st of Sept.

The good-natured inhabitants of Santiago have all testified, in some way or other, their sympathy with my sufferings. From the Director, who sent M. De la Salle with a very kind letter, in his own name and that of the ladies, to the poor nuns I had visited, who sent me a plate of excellent custard, made according to one of their own private recipes. . . .

24th

I have been better, and am much worse. My friend Mr Dance, from the *Doris*, arrived the day before yesterday with letters from every body on board, and a better account of poor Glennie. Mr. B. has interested himself to procure a comfortable caleche for me to travel to the port, as I am anxious to get home, and am not able to think of riding thither.

Nothing can be more truly kind than Doña Carmen de Cotapos and all her daughters, since I first became their guest, and especially since my illness. Mr Prevost too has been unwearied in his friendly attentions, but what can I say of my good and skilful physician Dr Craig, that can acknowledge my obligations sufficiently? As to my own sea friends, their affectionate care is only what I depended on. . . .

24 September – 12 November 1822

24th September

. . . It was not without regret that I left Santiago, where I have been so kindly received, and where there is still much new and interesting to see. I do hope to return in summer, when I mean to cross the mountain by the Cumbre pass, visit Mendoza, and return by the pass of San Juan de los Patos by which the great body of San Martin's army entered the country in 1816.

However, in the meantime I must gain a little more health, and a great deal more strength. I am scarcely sorry that I was obliged to travel in a caleche for once. All our party assembled after passing the toll-house, and other necessary ceremonies at the house of Loyola, the owner of the caleche, about a league from Santiago, on the plain called the Llomas. Sick as I felt, I could not help laughing at the 'set out'.

In the first place, there was the calisa, a very light square body of a carriage, mounted on a coarse heavy axle, and two clumsy wheels painted red, while the body is sprigged and flowered like a furniture chintz, lined with old yellow and red Chinese silk, without glasses, but having striped gingham curtains. Between the shafts, of the size and shape of those of a dung-cart, was a fine mule, not without silver studs among her trappings, mounted by a handsome lad in a poncho, and armed with spurs whose rowels were bigger than a dollar, and with a little straw hat stuck on one side. On each side of the mule was a horse, fastened to the axle of the wheel, each with his rider, also in full Chile costume.

Then there was Loyola's son as a guide, handsomely dressed in a full guaso dress, mounted on a fine horse, with him Mr Dance and Mr Candler, of the *Doris*, also in the same dress, my young friend de Roos having left us some days before on the expiration of his leave of absence. Last, though by no means least, in his own esteem, was my peon Felipe, with his three mules and the baggage, accompanied by another peon with the relay horses for the calisa. . . . The season is considerably advanced since we went to the city, the plains are thickly and richly covered with grass and flowers, the village orchards are in full leaf and blossom, and the pruning of the vines is begun. The horses, and other animals, are once more sent into the potreros to grass, and spring comes to all but me.

Mine is past, and my summer has been blighted, yet hope, blessed hope! remains, that the autumn of my days may at least be more tranquil.

I suffered a great deal the two first days on the road, but the third I felt sensibly better, and fancied myself almost well, when, at the first post-house from Valparaiso, I found Captain Spencer, with half-a-dozen of my young shipmates, whom he had good naturedly brought out to meet me, and among them poor Glennie.

We all made a cheerful luncheon together, and then rode to Valparaiso, my maid mounting her horse, and Glennie taking her place in the calisa.

At home I found Mr Hogan, and several other friends, waiting to welcome me. And truly I have seldom enjoyed rest so much as this night, when both mind and body reposed, as they have not done since I knew of Glennie's arrival in bad health. . . .

October 1st

. . . I have received many visits in the course of the day to congratulate me on my return, the most and the kindest from my naval friends; and I am particularly flattered by Lord Cochrane's coming with Captains Wilkinson and Crosbie, and Mr H. E. to tea. Before I could give it to them, an incident truly characteristic happened, we were obliged to wait while a man went to catch a cow with the laça* on the hill, to procure milk.

After what I had seen of the management of the dairy at M. Salinas', I could not wonder, and had nothing to do but sit patiently till the milk arrived, and my guests being older inhabitants of the country than I am, were equally resigned; and the interval was filled with pleasant conversation.

Maria and Lord Cochrane refrained from discussing politics over tea, but in fact since Maria's absence affairs at the port had deteriorated.

Anger among the crews of the Chile squadron at not being paid had by now led to a crisis, a malicious rumour going the rounds that the government had already paid out to Lord Cochrane the greater part of the money due to the men. Discontent with the government had been further exacerbated by the proposed new trade regulations planned by the

* Lasso.

Director's unpopular minister, Rodriguez. These included an extension of government monopolies and a further increase in taxes.

Meanwhile the situation in the navy was mirrored in the army where the government was refusing to honour arrears of pay, and where the Director had aggravated matters by replacing General Freire, popular Commander of the Army of the South. It was a decision he would soon have cause to regret.

8th

My pleasure in receiving the visits of my friends to-day, has been sadly damped by the increased sufferings of poor Glennie. These sufferings have met with sympathy, however, if not relief, in a quarter from which I scarcely looked for it, namely, from La Chavelita, the old lady of the flower-garden.

She appeared about four o'clock with a bundle of herbs, carried by a little serving boy, and stalking into the room with great dignity, her tall figure rendered still taller by a high-crowned black hat, she seated herself by the bedside, and began to question the patient as to his disease. She then turned to me, and told me she had brought some medicines, one of which she would administer immediately, and in order to prepare it desired me to procure some warm brandy.

This being done, she produced from her leathern pocket a piece of cocoa grease, and dipping it into the brandy, began to anoint G.'s shoulders with it, harangueing all the time on the intimate connection between the shoulders and the lungs, and saying that whoever wished to cure the latter should begin by cooling the former.

Having operated for a quarter of an hour, she suffered the patient to lie down, and taking a bundle of cachanlangue (*herb centaury*) from the boy, desired me to infuse half of it in boiling water, and give the tea occasionally, and the other half was to be placed in a glass of spirits, and the shoulders to be occasionally whipped with it.

She assured me that the pulse would go down and the hemorrhage cease by degrees, by constant use of the herb. She also gave me a bundle of wild carrot, of which she directed me to make a tisane, well sweetened, to be drank occasionally, and then, having given a history of similar cases cured by her prescriptions, to which she sometimes adds an infusion of the leaves of vinagrillo (*yellow wood-sorrel, with a thick fleshy leaf*), she took leave.

9th

One cannot attend to private concerns two days together. This morning I learn that the squadron is in such a state from want, that a delegate has been sent to the supreme government, and that the captains serving in the Chileno ships have addressed a serious letter to it, setting forth their claims, their sufferings, and the injustice done them.

In other respects, things are quieter, . . .

Lord Cochrane and Captain Crosbie came in the evening, and as we never talk politics while drinking tea and eating bread and honey, we had at least one pleasant hour without thinking of governments, or mutinies, or injustice of any kind – a rare blessing here, when two or three are together.

There are so few people here, and all those are so directly interested in these matters, that it is not wonderful nothing else should be talked of, but I, who am only a passenger, sometimes sigh for what I enjoyed this evening – a little rational conversation on more general topics. . . .

13th

Every one has been electrified to-day by the sudden arrival of General San Martin, the Protector of Peru, in this port.

Since the forcible expulsion of his minister and favourite, Monteagudo,* from office by the people of Lima,† while he himself was absent visiting Bolivar‡ at Guayaquil, he had felt some alarm concerning his own security, and had, it is believed, from time to time deposited considerable sums on board of the *Puyrredon*, in case of the worst.

At length, at midnight on the 20th September, he embarked, and ordered the captain to get under weigh instantly, although the vessel was not half manned, and had scarcely any water on board. He then ran down to Ancon, whence he despatched a messenger to Lima, and his impatience could scarcely brook the necessary delay before an answer could arrive, when it did come, he ordered the captain instantly to sail for Valparaiso, and now gives out here, that a rheumatic pain in one of his arms obliges him to have recourse to the baths of Cauquenes.

If true, "'tis strange, 'tis passing strange.'

* He was blamed for the persecution of colonial Spaniards in Lima.
† 25 July 1822.
‡ Simon Bolivar (1783–1830), leader of the revolution of Venezuela against Spain. Founded the republics of Colombia and Bolivia.

14th

Reports arrive this morning that San Martin has been arrested, and that having endeavoured to smuggle a quantity of gold, it is seized.

Noon

So far from San Martin being arrested, two of the Director's aides-de-camp have arrived to pay him compliments – besides, the fort saluted his flag.

Many persons, knowing Lord Cochrane's sentiments with regard to the General, and that he looks on him both as a traitor to Chile and a dishonest man, made little doubt but that His Lordship would arrest him. Had he done so, I think the government would have gladly acquiesced. But the uprightness and delicacy of Lord Cochrane's feelings have induced him to leave him to the government itself.

Night

The Director's carriage is arrived to convey San Martin to the city, General Priete and Major O'Carrol are also in attendance, and there are four orderlies appointed, who are never to lose sight of him. Some think by way of keeping him in honourable arrest, others, and I am inclined to be of the number, that real or affected fear for his life, while in the port, occasions the constant attendance of such a train.

The General himself persists in saying that his visit to Chile is solely on account of his rheumatic arm, and at first sight it seems hard not to allow a man credit for knowing the motives of his own actions. But one of the penalties of conspicuous station is to be judged by others. . . .

15th of October

After a very busy day spent in seeing and taking leave of my friends of the *Doris*, who are to sail to-morrow, I was surprised, just as I had taken leave of the last, at being told that a great company was approaching.

I had scarcely time to look up before I perceived Zenteno, the governor of Valparaiso, ushering in a very tall fine-looking man, dressed in plain black clothes, whom he announced as General San Martin. They were followed by Madame Zenteno and her step-daughter, Doña Dolores, Colonel D'Albe and his wife and sister, General Priete, Major O'Carrol, Captain Torres, who I believe is captain of the port here, and two other gentlemen whom I do not know.

It was not easy to arrange the seats of such a company in a room scarcely sixteen feet square, and lumbered with books and other things necessary to the comfort of an European woman. At length, however, my occupation of much serving being over, I could sit, and observe, and listen.

San Martin's eye has a pecularity in it that I never saw before but once, and that was in the head of a celebrated lady.

It is dark and fine, but restless, it never seemed to fix for above a moment, but that moment expressed every thing. His countenance is decidedly handsome, sparkling, and intelligent, but *not open*. His manner of speaking quick, but often obscure, with a few tricks and by-words, but a great flow of language, and a readiness to talk on all subjects.

I am not fond of recording even the topics of private conversation, which I think ought always to be sacred. But San Martin is not a private man, and besides, the subjects were general, not personal.

We spoke of government, and there I think his ideas are far from being either clear or decisive.

There seems a timidity of intellect, which prevents the daring to give freedom and the daring to be despotic alike. The wish to enjoy the reputation of a liberator and the will to be a tyrant are strangely contrasted in his discourse. He has not read much, nor is his genius of that stamp that can go alone. Accordingly, he continually quoted authors whom he evidently knew but by halves, and of the half he knew he appeared to me to mistake the spirit.

When we spoke of religion, and Zenteno joined in the discourse, he talked much of philosophy, and both those gentlemen seemed to think that philosophy consisted in leaving religion to the priests and to the vulgar, as a state-machine, while the wise man would laugh alike at the monk, the protestant, and the deist. Well does Bacon say, 'None deny there is a God but those for whom it maketh that there were no God' and truly, when I consider his actions, I feel that he should be an atheist if he would avoid despair.

But I am probably too severe on San Martin. His natural shrewd sense must have led him to perceive the absurdity of the Roman Catholic superstitions, which here are naked in their ugliness, not glossed over with the pomp and elegance of Italy, and which from state policy he has often joined in with all outward demonstrations of respect.

It has been observed, that 'The Roman Catholic system is shaken off with much greater difficulty than those which are taught in the reformed churches, but when it loses its hold of the mind, it much more frequently prepares the way for unlimited scepticism.' And this appears to me to be exactly the state of San Martin's mind. From religion, and the changes it has undergone from corruptions and from reformations, the transition was easy to political revolutions.

The reading of all South American reformers is mostly in a French channel, and the age of Louis xiv was talked of as the direct and only cause of the French revolution, and consequently of those in South America. A slight compliment was thrown in to King William* before I had ventured to observe, that perhaps the former evils and present good of these countries might in part be traced to the wars of Charles v† and his successor, draining these provinces of money, and returning nothing. . . .

I was glad of the interruption afforded by the entrance of tea to this somewhat pedantic discourse, which I never should have made a note of but that it was San Martin's. I apologized for having no matee to offer, but I found that both the General and Zenteno drank tea without milk, with their segars in preference.

But the interruption even of tea, stopped San Martin but for a short time. Resuming the discourse, he talked of physic, of language, of climate, of diseases, and that not delicately, and lastly, of antiquities, especially those of Peru, and told some very marvellous stories of the perfect preservation of some whole families of ancient Caciques and Incas who had buried themselves alive on the Spanish invasion. This brought us to far the most interesting part of his discourse – his own leaving Lima.

He told me, that, resolved to know whether the people were really happy, he used to disguise himself in a common dress, and, like the caliph Haroun Alraschid, to mingle in the coffee-houses, and in the gossiping parties at the shop doors, that he often heard himself spoken of, and gave me to understand, that he had found that the people were now happy enough to do without him.

He said that, after the active life he had led, he began to wish for rest, that he had withdrawn from public life, satisfied that his part was accomplished, and that he had only brought with him the flag of Pizarro.

This was the banner under which the empire of the Incas had been conquered, and which had been displayed in every war, not only those between the Spaniards and Peruvians, but those of the rival Spanish chiefs.

* William III (1650–1702) King of England.
† Emperor Charles V (1500–58) Hapsburg Emperor.

'*Its possession,*' said he, '*has always been considered the mark of power and authority, I HAVE IT NOW*', and he drew himself up to his full height, and looked round him with a most imperial air.

Nothing so characteristic as this passed during the whole four hours the Protector remained with me. It was the only moment in which he was himself. The rest was partly an habitual talking on all subjects, to dazzle the less understanding, and partly the impatience to be first, even in common conversation, which his long habit of command has given him.

I pass over the compliments* he paid me, somewhat too profusely for the occasion, but of such we may say, as Johnson did of affectation, that they are excusable, because they proceed from the laudable desire of pleasing.

Indeed, his whole manner was most courteous. I could not but observe, that his movements as well as his person are graceful, and I can well believe what I have heard, that in a ball-room he has few superiors.

Of the other persons present, Colonel d'Albe and the ladies only volunteered a few words. It was with difficulty that, in my endeavours to be polite to all, I forced a syllable now and then from the other gentlemen. They seemed as if afraid to commit themselves, so at length I left them alone, and the whole discourse soon fell into the Protector's hands.

Upon the whole, the visit of this evening has not impressed me much in favour of San Martin. His views are narrow, and I think selfish. His philosophy, as he calls it, and his religion, are upon a par, both are too openly used as mere masks to impose on the world, and, indeed, they are so worn as that they would not impose on any people but those he has unhappily had to rule.

He certainly has no genius, but he has some talents, with no learning, and little general knowledge. Of that little, however, he has the dexterity to make a great deal of use, nobody possesses more of that most useful talent, 'l'art de se faire valoir'.

His fine person, his air of superiority, and that suavity of manner which has so long enabled him to lead others, give him very decided advantages. He understands English, and speaks French tolerably, and I know no person with whom it might be pleasanter to pass half an hour, but the want of heart, and the want of candour, which are evident even in conversation of any length, would never do for intimacy, far less for friendship.

* One regrets Maria's modesty. It would have been interesting to know why San Martin wanted to impress her. Perhaps not only because she was a friend of his rival, Lord Cochrane.

At nine o'clock the party left me, much pleased certainly at having seen one of the most remarkable men in South America, and I think that, perhaps, in the time, I saw as much of him as was possible. He aims at universality, in imitation of Napoleon, who had, I have heard, something of that weakness, and whom he is always talking of as his model, or rather rival. I think too that he had a mind to exhibit himself to me as a stranger, or Zenteno might have suggested, that even the little additional fame that my report of him could give was worth the trouble of seeking. The fact certainly is, that he did talk to-night for display. . . .

17th

Mr Clarke called on his way to the city, and brought me San Martin's farewell to Peru. It is as follows:–

> I have been present at the declaration of the independence of the states of Chile and of Peru. The standard which Pizarro brought hither to enslave the empire of the Incas is in my power. I have ceased to be a public man: thus I am rewarded with usury for ten years of revolution and war.
>
> My promises to the countries where I have made war are fulfilled, – to make them independent, and to leave them to the free choice of their government.
>
> The presence of a fortunate soldier (however disinterested I may be) is terrible to newly constituted states; and besides, I am shocked at hearing it said that I desire to make myself a sovereign. Nevertheless, I shall always be ready to make the last sacrifice for the liberty of the country; but in the rank of a simple individual, *and no other*.
>
> As to my public conduct, my countrymen, as in most things, will be divided in their opinions: their posterity will pronounce a true sentence.
>
> Peruvians! I leave you an established national representation: if you repose entire confidence in it, sing your song of triumph; if not, anarchy will devour you.
>
> May prudence preside over your destinies; and may these crown you with happiness and peace!
>
> JOSE DE SAN MARTIN

Pueblo Libro, Sept. 20th, 1822.

If there be any thing real in this, if he really retires and troubles the world no more, he will merit at least such praise as was bestowed on

> The Roman, when his burning heart
> Was slaked with blood of Rome,

> Threw down his dagger, dared depart
> In savage grandeur home:
> He dared depart in utter scorn
> Of men that such a yoke had borne.

For indeed he has not 'held his faculties meekly'; but yet he has done something for the good cause; – and oh! had the means been righteous as the cause, he would have been the very first of his countrymen: but there is blood on his hands; there is the charge of treachery on his heart.

16th

He is this day gone to Cauquenes, and has left the port not one whit enlightened as to the cause of his leaving Peru. It is probably like the retirement of Monteagudo, a sacrifice of his political existence in order to save his natural life.

I think Lord Cochrane went either to-day or yesterday to Quintero. The Valparaiso world would have rejoiced in some meeting, some scene, between him and San Martin, but his good sense, and truly honourable feelings towards the country he serves, have prevented this.

If San Martin is unfortunate, and forced to fly his dominion, His Lordship's conduct is magnanimous, if it be only a *ruse de guerre* on San Martin's part to save himself, it is prudent, and will leave him at liberty to expose the Protector as he deserves. . . .

October 31st

This month has been a most important one for Chile. The government has promulgated its new constitution and its new commercial regulations, neither of which appear to me to answer their purpose. . . .

November 1st

My invalid is now so much better, that we have been riding out upon the hills, and getting acquainted with new paths and new flowers. Poor fellow! he seems more delighted at his renewed liberty even than I am at mine. . . .

2d

We have had a great many visitors, and of course some news, the most interesting of which is, that the government is in earnest in its intentions to pay the squadron. One half of the payments will, it is said, be made in money, the other half in bills upon the custom-house.

Lord Cochrane arrived from the city last night, and is pitching tents by the sea-shore beyond the fort for himself, because he does not choose to accept a house from government, in the way these things are managed here. He has of course a claim to the accommodation of a dwelling on shore, and an order was sent to the governor of Valparaiso to provide one.

The governor consequently pitched upon one of the most commodious in the port, and sent an order to Mr C., an Englishman, to remove with his family, and to leave it furnished for the Admiral, such being the old Spanish custom. But His Lordship would by no means allow Mr C. to move, and has accordingly pitched a tent. His friends are a little anxious about this step. No Chileno would lift his hand against him, but there are persons now in Chile who hate him, and who have both attempted and committed assassination.

Sunday, November 3d

This evening, at about nine o'clock, the Director came quietly to the port. It is said he is come to see the squadron paid. Some assert that he is come in order not immediately to meet San Martin, who, having bathed at Cauquenes, is about to move into the city, and is to take up his residence in the directorial palace, only, however, as a private visitor. He is to have a double guard, but if he is, as it is said, so beloved, why should he fear? I suspect that, like other opium-eaters, he is become nervous.

I trust, for the honour of human nature, that an opinion which I have heard concerning the Director's appearance in the port, is unfounded. It is, that he is come hither in order to seize an opportunity of getting possession of Lord Cochrane's person, that is, to sacrifice him to the revenge of San Martin in compliance with the entreaties forwarded from Peru, by the agents Paroissien* and Del Rio.

* It was Paroissien who had filed complaints against Lord Cochrane for the Chilean government.

November 7th

We have been riding about for several days, and making acquaintance among the neighbouring farmers, every where we are invited to alight and take milk, or at least to rest, and walk in the gardens and gather flowers. It is quite refreshing to see the gentle and frank manners of the peasants of the country, after all the bustle and petty intrigue of the port and its in-dwellers.

To-day, however, I have spent very agreeably to myself, chiefly at the Admiral's tents, but that is far enough from the town not to hear its noise. Having lodged Glennie at the tents, I returned to the town and called on the Director, who is living in the government-house, and Zenteno and his family are gone to another. His Excellency looks very well, and received me as courteously as I could wish, and according to the custom of the country, as soon as I was seated presented me with a flower.

I know not how it happened, but the discourse turned on nunneries, and I mentioned the Philippine nuns in Rome, on which he begged to have a particular notice of them and their rule, in order to better the condition, if possible, of the nuns of Chile, and especially of such as superintend the education of young girls. This I promised. . . .

Having paid my visits, I returned to the tents, and found that my patient had been sleeping quietly. Lord Cochrane, much interested in him, kindly pressed me to take him for change of air to Quintero, which I am most willing to do, and as soon as he is strong enough, I mean to go.

The Admiral himself does not look very well, but that is not marvellous, the squadron is still unpaid. The charges preferred against him by San Martin, though never credited by the government, which possesses abundant documents in its own hands to refute them, have remained uncontradicted by him, at the request of that government, in order to avoid exciting party spirit, or a quarrel, perhaps a war, between Peru and Chile.

But now that all danger of that kind is over, and as San Martin is honoured by having the palace itself appointed for his residence, and receives every mark of public attention (as if on purpose to insult Lord Cochrane), those charges should and will be answered. And answered too with facts and dates which will completely overwhelm all the accusations, direct and indirect, that were ever drawn up or insinuated against him.

There are other causes too why those now in high station in Chile should be anxious. There are reports and whispers from the north and from the south, of discontents of various kinds. The brothers and kindred of the dead, and of the exiled, have not forgotten them, and to see the man whom they consider as the author of their misfortunes received and honoured irritates them.

With every respect for the personal character of the Director, they see him as the friend and ally of San Martin, and the supporter of Rodriguez and his comrades, and I can hear that sort of covert voice of discontent that precedes civil strife.

The government of Santiago throws all the blame of this discontent on the squadron, and has sent a few troops here, it is said, to intimidate it, but the number is so small, that it would scarcely suffice to guard the Director, or to secure a state prisoner, to which latter purpose those who best know the dispositions of the government believe them to be destined.

The Admiral is undoubtedly the person who would be seized, if the partisans of San Martin dared commit so great an outrage. Nor would they stop there. San Martin's victims never survive his grasp. I am grieved that the Director should lend himself to such a purpose. The people in the port seeming not to dare to speak, say in fact every thing, and I was glad to take refuge from hearing disagreeable things at the tents, where, at least, we are secure from hearing of the politics of Chile.

12th

I may say, with the North Americans, every thing is *progressing*; Glennie is much better; the discontents are spreading. The squadron is in a way to be paid, though, perhaps, too late. . . . I have received a letter from the Director in answer to mine about the nuns. . . . Lord Cochrane is proceeding with his refutation of San Martin; and I have seen him, and fixed on a time for being at Quintero. . . .

20 November 1822 – 18 January 1823

Maria and Glennie set out for Quintero a week later. At midday they broke their journey at Vina la Mar, the hacienda belonging to cousins of the Carreras, so that Glennie could rest, then rode on to Concon* where they were met by the Miers family.

The spent the night with the Miers, and by the 17th were at Quintero where Mr Bennet, Lord Cochrane's secretary, and Carillo, a painter friend of Maria's, were waiting to greet them.

Here one of the first things Maria did was to make a sketch of the house, 'having found a lithographic press here, I mean to draw it on stone, and so produce the first print of any kind that has been drawn in Chile, or, I believe, on this side of South America'.[1]

November 20th

Yesterday, after dinner, Glennie having fallen into a sound sleep in his arm-chair by the fire side, Mr Bennet and I, attracted by the fineness of the evening, took our seats to the veranda overlooking the bay, and, for the first time since my arrival in Chile, I saw it lighten. The lightning continued to play uninterruptedly over the Andes until after dark, when a delightful and calm moonlight night followed a quiet and moderately warm day.

We returned reluctantly to the house on account of the invalid, and were sitting quietly conversing, when, at a quarter past ten, the house received a violent shock, with a noise like the explosion of a mine.

Mr Bennet starting up, ran out, exclaiming, 'An earthquake, an earthquake! for God's sake follow me!'

I, feeling more for Glennie than any thing, and fearing the night air for him, sat still. He, looking at me to see what I would do, did the same, until, the vibration still increasing, the chimneys fell, and I saw the walls of the house open.

Mr Bennet again cried from without, 'For God's sake, come away from the house!'

So we rose and went to the veranda, meaning, of course, to go by the steps. But the vibration increased with such violence, that

* The Miers' estate.

133

hearing the fall of a wall behind us, we jumped down from the little platform to the ground, and were scarcely there, when the motion of the earth changed from a quick vibration to a rolling like that of a ship at sea, so that it was with difficulty that Mr Bennet and I supported Glennie.

The shock lasted three minutes, and, by the time it was over, every body in and about the house had collected on the lawn, excepting two persons. One, the wife of a mason, who was shut up in a small room which she could not open, the other Carillo, who, in escaping from his room by the wall which fell, was buried in the ruins, but happily preserved by the lintel falling across him.

Never shall I forget the horrible sensation of that night. In all other convulsions of nature we feel or fancy that some exertion may be made to avert or mitigate danger, but from an earthquake there is neither shelter nor escape. The 'mad disquietude' that agitates every heart, and looks out in every eye, seems to me as awful as the last judgment can be, and I regret that my anxiety for my patient overcoming other feelings, I had not my due portion of that sublime terror. But I looked round and I saw it.

Amid the noise of the destruction before and around us, I heard the lowings of the cattle all the night through, and I heard too the screaming of the sea-fowl, which ceased not till morning. There was not a breath of air, yet the trees were so agitated, that their topmost branches seemed on the point of touching the ground.

It was some time ere our spirits recovered so as to ask each other what was to be done, but we placed Glennie, who had had a severe hemorrhage from the lungs instantly, under a tree in an arm-chair. I stood by him while Mr B[ennet] entered the house and procured spirits and water, of which we all took a little, and a tent was then pitched for the sick man, and we fetched out a sofa and blankets for him. Then I got a man to hold a light, and venture with me to the inner rooms to fetch medicine.

A second and a third shock had by this time taken place, but so much less violent than the first, that we had reasonable hopes that the worst was over, and we proceeded through the ruined sitting-rooms to cross the court where the wall had fallen, and as we reached the top of the ruins, another smart shock seemed to roll them from under our feet.

At length we reached the first door of the sleeping apartments, and on entering I saw the furniture displaced from the walls, but paid little attention to it. In the second room, however, the disorder, or rather the displacing, was more striking, and then it seemed to me that there was a regularity in the disposal of every thing. This was still more apparent in my own room, and after having got the medicines and bedding I went for, I observed the furniture in the different rooms, and found that it had all been moved in the same direction. (This morning I took in my compass, and found that direction to be north-west and south-east.) The night still continued serene, and though the moon went down early, the sky was light, and there was a faint aurora australis.

Having made Glennie lie down in the tent, I put my mattress on the ground by him. Mr Bennet, and the overseer, and the workmen, lay down with such bedding as they could get round the tent. It was now twelve o'clock, the earth was still at unrest, and shocks, accompanied by noises like the explosion of gunpowder, or rather like those accompanying the jets of fire from a volcano, returned every two minutes. I lay with my watch in my hand counting them for forty-five minutes, and then, wearied out, I fell asleep. But a little before two o'clock a loud explosion and tremendous shock roused every one, and a horse and a pig broke loose, and came to take refuge among us.

At four o'clock there was another violent shock, and the interval had been filled with a constant trembling, with now and then a sort of cross-motion, the general direction of the undulations being north and south. At a quarter past six o'clock there was another shock, which at another time would have been felt severely.

Since that hour, though there has been a continued series of agitations, such as to shake and even spill water from a glass, and though the ground is still trembling under me, there has been nothing to alarm us. *I write at four o'clock p.m.*

At daylight I went out of the tent to look at the earth. The dew was on the grass, and all looked as beautiful as if the night's agitation had not taken place, but here and there cracks of various sizes appeared in various parts of the hill. At the roots of the trees, and the bases of the posts supporting the veranda, the earth appeared separate, so that I could put my hand in, and had the appearance of earth where the gardener's dibble had been used.

By seven o'clock persons from various quarters had arrived, either to enquire after our fate, or communicate their own. From Valle Alegri, a village on the estate, we hear that many, even of the peasants' houses, are damaged, and some destroyed. In various places in the middle of the gardens, the earth has cracked, and water and sand have been forced up through the surface. Some banks have fallen in, and the watercourses are much injured.

Mr Cruikshank has ridden over from old Quintero. He tells us that great fissures are made on the banks of the lake, the house is not habitable, some of its inmates were thrown down by the shock, and others by the falling of various articles of furniture upon them. At Concon the whole house is unroofed, the walls cracked, the iron supporters broken, the mill a ruin, and the banks of the mill-stream fallen in. . . .

Half past eight p.m. – We hear reports that the large and populous town of Quillota, is a heap of ruins, and that Valparaiso is little better. If so, the destruction there must have reached to the inhabitants as well as the houses – God forbid it should be so!

At a quarter before six another very serious shock, and one this moment. Slight shocks occur every fifteen or twenty minutes.

The evening is as fine as possible, the moon is up, and shines beautifully over the lake and the bay. The stars and aurora australis are also brilliant, and a soft southerly breeze has been blowing since daylight.

We have erected a large rancho with bamboo from Guayaquil and reeds from the lake, so that we can eat and sleep under cover. Glennie and I keep the tent, the rest sleep in the rancho.

Thursday, November 21st

At half past two a.m. I was awoke, by a severe shock. At ten minutes before three a tremendous one, which made us feel anew that utter helplessness which is so appalling. At a quarter before eight, another not so severe. A quarter past nine, another. At half past ten and a quarter past one, they were repeated. One at twenty minutes before two with very loud noise, lasting a minute and a half, and the last remarkable one to-day at a quarter past ten.

These were all that were in any degree alarming, but slight shocks occurred every twenty or thirty minutes.

Mr M[iers] is returned from the port. Lord Cochrane was on board the *O'Higgins* at the time of the first great shock, and went on shore instantly to the Director for whom he got a tent pitched on the hill behind the town.

His Lordship writes me that my cottage is still standing, though every thing round is in ruins. Mr M[iers] says that there is not a house standing whole in the Almendral. The church of the Merced is quite destroyed.

Not one house in the port remains habitable, though many retain their forms. There is not a living creature to be seen in the streets, but the hills are covered with wretches driven from their homes, and whose mutual fears keep up mutual distraction.

The ships in the harbour are crowded with people, no provisions are to be had, the ovens are ruined, and the bakers cannot work.

Five English persons were killed, and they were digging out some of the natives, but the loss of life has not been so great as might have been feared. Had the catastrophe happened later, when the people had retired to bed, the destruction must have been very dreadful. . . .

Friday, November 22d

Three severe shocks at a quarter past four, at half past seven, and at nine o'clock.

After that there were three loud explosions, with slight trembling between, then a severe shock at eleven, two or three very slight before one o'clock, and then we had a respite until seven p.m., when there was a slight shock.

As we are thirty miles from the port, and ninety from the city, the reports come to us but slowly. To-day, however, we learn that Santiago is less damaged than we expected.

The mint has suffered seriously, part of the directorial palace has fallen, the houses and churches are in some instances cracked through, but no serious damage is done, excepting the breaking down the canals for irrigation in some places.

A gentleman from Valparaiso describes the sensation experienced on board the ships as being as if they had suddenly got under weigh and gone along with violence, striking on rocks as they went.

Last night, the priests had prophesied a more severe shock than the first. No one went to bed, all that could huddle themselves and goods on board any vessel did so, and the hills were covered with groups of houseless creatures, sitting round the fires in awful expectation of a mighty visitation. . . .

Such are our reports from a distance. Nearer home we have had the same prophecy, concerning a greater shock with an inundation to be expected, and the peasants consequently abandoned their dwellings, and fled to the hills.

The shock did not arrive, and that it did not has been attributed to the interposition of Our Lady of Quintero. This same Lady of Quintero has a chapel at the old house, and her image there has long been an object of peculiar veneration.

Thither, on the first dreadful night, flocked all the women of the neighbourhood, and with shrieks and cries entreated her to come to their assistance, tearing their hair, and calling her by all the endearing names which the church of Rome permits to the objects of its worship.

She came not forth, however, and in the morning, when the priests were able to force the doors obstructed by the fallen rubbish, they found her prostrate, with her head off, and several fingers broken. It was not long, however, before she was restored to her pristine state, dressed in clean clothes, and placed in the attitude of benediction before the door of her shattered fane.*

We had a thick fog to-day, and a cold drizzling rain all the morning till noon, when it cleared up, and became still and warm.

During many of the shocks, I observed wine or water on the table was not agitated by a regular tremulous motion, but appeared suddenly thrown up in heaps. On the surface of the water, in one large decanter, I observed three such heaps form and suddenly subside, as if dashing against the sides. Mercury, in a decanter, was affected in the same manner. We had no barometer with us, nor could I learn that any observations had been made. . . .

On 24 November shocks were registered at eight a.m. and again at three, five and eleven p.m., though Maria recorded that she didn't feel the first, since, by six in the morning, she was already on her way to Valparaiso.

She halted briefly at Concon to see the Miers, whose house had been almost completely destroyed. They themselves had only just escaped with their lives, and were now forced to shelter in a makeshift hut of branches.

At Vina a la Mar, nothing was standing, and the family huddled together by one of their outer gateways, while all the way between them and the port Maria's sure-footed little horse had to pick his way through debris.

On reaching the hill above Valparaiso all at first looked normal, then she noticed the absence of church spires and the higher buildings, but it was only when she approached the town that the extent of the calamity was revealed in the miserable tents of the refugees, 'Rich and poor, young and old, masters and servants, were huddled together in intimacy frightful even here, where the distinction of rank is by no means so broad as in Europe.'[2]

When she reached her own house she was amazed to find the only damage was fourteen tiles off the roof.

'Seeing that my house was in a manner untouched, the priests resolved to make a miracle of it, and accordingly by daylight on the twentieth, Nuestra Señora del Pilar was found, in her satin gown, standing close to my stove, and received numerous offerings for having protected the premises, and I suppose carried off a silver pocket-compass and a smelling bottle, the only two things I missed!'[3]

* Temple.

Monday, 25th

So severe a shock took place at a quarter past eight o'clock this morning, as to shake down a great deal of what had been spared on the night of the 19th. Two others occurred in the course of the forenoon, and two after seven at night.

I have been busy all day packing my books, clothes, &c., to remove, because my house is let over my head to some persons who, seeing how well it has stood, have bribed the landlord to let it to them. – *They are English!*

While I was thus busy, Lord Cochrane called, with Captain Crosbie. His Lordship most kindly, most humanely, desired me to remain at Quintero, with my poor invalid, and not to think of removing him or myself until more favourable times and circumstances, and told me he would soon go thither, and settle whereabouts I should shelter myself and Glennie till he should be well enough finally to remove.

Tuesday, 26th

There were five shocks during this day: I must now omit many; because, unless they are very severe, I never awake in consequence of them during the night. . . .

Mr C. has indeed, however, brought intelligence more important than any thing connected with the earthquake. The people of Conception, enraged at the unjust provisions of the reglamento, and at other oppressive measures,* have burnt the same reglamento and the constitution in the market-place, have convoked an opposition convention, and have insisted on Freire's taking the field with the acknowledged purpose of turning out Rodriguez and the rest of the iniquitous administration. Freire has already marched, but as yet his motions cannot be known at Santiago, and of course I am tongue-tied as to the intelligence, till it comes from some public quarter. Conjecture is free, however, and I cannot help thinking that the object here has been to secure the squadron in Freire's interest.

But that may not be, honour forbids it, I think; and the Chilian squadron will not forget honour, while its present chief† is even nominally its admiral.

---

* Taxes and monopolies.
† Lord Cochrane.

Wednesday, 27th

Several slight shocks to-day: a very severe one at ten o'clock a.m., and again at six p.m. . . .

I intended to have returned to Quintero to-day, the launch of the *Lautaro** having been obligingly lent to me for that purpose. But, contrary to all experience at this time of the year, a strong northerly wind set in, which totally prevented it. At night a heavy torrent of rain fell, which has done great damage by injuring the goods left exposed by the falling of the houses, and which has rendered the miserable encampments on the hills thoroughly wretched.

Yet the people are rejoicing at it, because they say that the rain will extinguish the fire that causes the earthquake, and we shall have no more.

28th

Notwithstanding the rain, which lasted till midnight, we have experienced no less than five shocks to-day. . . .

I went on board the Admiral's ship soon after breakfast to call on some of my friends, who, with their families, had taken refuge there on the night of the 19th, and to whom he had given up his cabin and lived himself in a tent on deck.

The officers with whom I talked on the effect of the earthquake on board, told me, that, on feeling the shock and hearing the horrid noise, compounded of the aweful sound from the earth itself and that of the falling town, they had looked towards the land, and had seen only one cloud of dust and heard one dreadful shriek.

Lord Cochrane and others threw themselves immediately into a boat, to go to the assistance, if help were still possible, of the sufferers. The rushing wave landed them higher than any boat had been before, and they then saw it retire frightfully, and leave many of the launches and other small vessels dry.

They fully expected a return, and the probable drowning of the town, but the water came back no more, and the whole bottom of the bay has risen about three feet. Every one had some peculiar escape to relate. . . .

After spending a very interesting forenoon on board the *O'Higgins*, listening to these tales of terror, I returned to Quintero in the *Lautaro*'s launch, which performed the voyage in three

* One of the ships of the Chileno squadron.

hours, and might have done it in less, but for the swell, the consequence of yesterday's north wind.

29th

Only one very sensible shock to-day. . . .

Dec. 2d

We have felt but one shock early this morning. . . . and though we . . . are living in tents and huts pitched round our ruined dwelling, we pursue our business, and even our amusements, as if nothing had happened, and lie down to sleep as confidently as if we had not lately seen the earth whereon we repose reeling to and fro. . . .

The southern winds are now come, and they often bring us such clouds of dust that our attempts to write are in vain, and our food would be defiled did we not retire to a little bower under the shelter of a hill. Here, in a dining-room of Nature's own making, with its door and windows looking to the ocean complete, we eat and remain until the evening calm comes on, when we collect round a large fire that we burn at the front of our tents, and talk till bed time. . . .

Tuesday, December 3d

The earth, which seemed to have resumed its stillness, has this day been violently convulsed. At half past three a.m., at nine, at noon, a long and very severe shock with much noise. At two o'clock another. At midnight a fifth, not inferior to those of the three first days, always excepting the first great one. . . .

Friday, 6th

Only two shocks, but the highest wind I remember. A beautifully bright day, and the bay as lovely as possible, with the white waves dashing over the dark-blue surface.

We were obliged to take shelter in the grove, as the showers of sand penetrate the rancho in every direction, and nearly suffocate us.

I have tied the branches of the quintral that hangs from the maytens to the shrubs below, and so made our wall firmer, and our window more shapely, that we may look out upon the sea and the hills. And having stuck four posts into the earth, and laid one of the

141

fallen doors upon them, we are furnished with an admirable dining-table.

December 7th

. . . Lord Cochrane arrived in the *Montezuma* with Captain Winter and Messrs Grenfell and Jackson. Glennie, who appeared to have been gaining ground for a fortnight, had another attack to-day. . . .

Monday, 9th

One very slight shock. The day dull and cloudy. The thermometer at 65° Fahrenheit. In the evening I had a pleasant walk to the beach with Lord Cochrane. We went chiefly for the purpose of tracing the effects of the earthquake along the rocks. . . .

Tuesday, 10th

While sitting at dinner with Lord Cochrane, Messrs Jackson, Bennet, and Orelle, we were startled by the longest and severest shock since the first great earthquake of the 19th November.

Some ran out of the house (for we now inhabit a part of it), and I flew to poor Glennie's bed-side. It had brought on severe hemorrhage, which I stopped with laudanum. Soon afterwards we had a slighter shock, and again at half past three a severe one. The wind was most violent, the thermometer at 65°. . . .

From now on in ominous counterpoint nature herself seemed to combine with the increasingly disturbing political developments.

On the 17th they heard General Freire had advanced as far as Talca and that a division of the army of Santiago had been ordered in readiness to meet him. Meanwhile there were rumours that the Galvarino *had been made ready for sea to take some important personage (possibly San Martin) to safety.*

'We begin to feel the anxieties preparatory to a civil war,' wrote Maria. 'Our pistols are cleaned, we have prepared a store of bullets . . .'[4]

Three days later, ignoring further earthquake shocks she again rode from Quintero to Valparaiso, musing as she went, 'Earthquake under me, civil war around me, my poor sick relation apparently dying, and my kind friend, my only friend here indeed, certainly going to leave the country, at least for a time.'[5]

This was of course Lord Cochrane, who, probably unknown to Maria, had been approached by Don Pedro of Brazil to do for Brazil, what he had already accomplished for Chile – the freeing of their ports from the navy of the mother country.

On arrival at Valparaiso Maria conducted some business at the port, changed her riding dress and went on board the O'Higgins to dine with Lord Cochrane.

Here she learned that though he had twice tendered his resignation to the Chilean government, it had not been accepted, but that nevertheless he was still resolved on what he called 'a temporary absence' from the country – a voyage in fact to Brazil, whose offer of employment he had by now accepted.

The news clearly depressed Maria, for after dinner as she was leaning on the taffrail pondering the difficulties of her situation and the dreariness of her prospects, Lord Cochrane came up 'and gently calling my attention, said, that as he was going to sail soon from this country, I should take a great uneasiness from his mind if I would go with him.

'He could not bear, he said, to leave the unprotected widow of a British officer thus on the beach, and cast away as it were in a ruined town, a country full of civil war!

'I replied, I could not leave my sick relation – I had promised his mother to watch him.

' "Nor do I ask you to do so," answered Lord Cochrane. "No, he must go too, and surely he will be as well taken care of with us, as you could do it alone."

'I could not answer – I could not look my thanks, but if there is anyone who has had an oppressive weight on the heart, that seemed too great either to bear or to obtain relief for, and who has had that weight suddenly and kindly removed, then they may understand my sensations . . .'[6]

She at once began preparations for the coming voyage, staying in Valparaiso for the purpose, though sleeping on board the O'Higgins like the other English, who, to avoid the earthquake shocks, had either hired whole ships or cabins in which to live.

On 23 December the launch of the Lautaro took her back to Quintero along with her purchases which included ingredients for a large Christmas pudding.

On Christmas Day the growing family at Quintero experienced a tremendous earthquake shock, almost as strong as the great shock of 19 November, and on the same day they heard that the people of Coquimbo had rejected the rule of the Director and were preparing to overturn the government in Santiago.

The government itself was fighting for its life, and in an attempt to give an impression of stability had issued orders for the rebuilding of Valparaiso, for which magnificent plans were projected. At the same time long overdue repairs were begun on both the O'Higgins and the Valdivia,

Lord Cochrane transferring his flag to the schooner Montezuma, *now the only serviceable ship in Valparaiso.*

Meanwhile at Quintero the oddly mixed band of friends, refugees and servants were living partly in the ruins of the Admiral's house, and partly in tents, rather after the manner of the shipwrecked courtiers in The Tempest.

'After dinner we generally walk to the sea-side to enjoy the prospect and the music of the sea, which comes "like the joys that are past, sweet and mournful to the soul",' wrote Maria, adding that they'd sat on the promontory of the Herradura to watch the last sun of 1822 go down into the Pacific. . . .[7]

By now Lord Cochrane had rearranged his guests in tents strung out along the sea-shore. 'The sea reaches to within a few yards of our tents, rolling smoothly in, just opposite and breaking a little to the left round the rocks and the wreck of the Aquila, *one of the Admiral's Guayaquil prizes. The shellfish have already taken possession of her, within and without,'*[8] *wrote Maria, adding that she'd sent her maid to take care of the Miers children, 'she was of no use here, and I did not think the sort of Robin Hood* life we are leading, the most advisable thing in the world for a young good-looking girl.'*[9]

She herself was engaged in setting up the lithographic press in Lord Cochrane's tent on which to print his rousing (though still 'temporary') farewell to the Chilenos.

'Chilenos,' it concluded, 'you know that independence is purchased at the point of the bayonet, know also that liberty is founded on good faith, and on the laws of honour; and that those who infringe upon them are your only enemies, among whom you will never find

Cochrane.'[10]

January 3d

. . . I like this wild life we are living, half in the open air. Every thing is an incident, and as we never know who is to come, or what is to happen next, we have the constant stimulus of curiosity to bear us to the end of every day.

The evening walk is the only thing we are sure of. Sometimes we trace the effects of the recent earthquake, and fancy they lead to marks of others infinitely more violent, and at periods long anterior to our knowledge. Often we have little other object than the mere pleasure of the earth, and air, and sky. Sometimes we go to the garden, where every thing is thriving beyond all hope. And

---

* Is this a slip for Robinson Crusoe?

we are busy collecting seeds of the wild plants of the country, though it is too early in the season to find many ripe.

5th

We have again lost the Admiral for a few days. The press is removed to my tent, where we are more free to work at all hours, without interrupting business or being interrupted by it . . .

10th

Lord Cochrane returned to us in the *Montezuma*. Every thing is finally settled as to our departure. The brig *Colonel Allen* is to come to Quintero, where we are all to embark, and in less than a week we expect to be under weigh.

All hands are now employed. The overseer's people on the hill salting beef, the carpenters nailing up boxes, people cutting strips of hide for cordage, secretaries writing, the press at work, sailors fitting spars across the light logs, called balsas, to make a raft to ship the goods with. And amidst all this, people coming and going, foreigners and English, to take leave of the Admiral, and some, I am sorry to say, for the purpose of being, and showing themselves, ungrateful. . . .

However, some in this country, and those among the best, have, I really think, a sincere regard for the Admiral. But I believe in friendship as in love, 'ce n'est pas tout d'être aimé; il faut être apprécié', and I scarcely know one here who is capable of appreciating him justly, so that even the very homage he receives is unworthy of him. Oh, why is he not at home!

17th

At length every thing is embarked, and we are ready to sail.

This morning I walked with Lord Cochrane to the tops of most of the hills immediately between the house of the Herradura and the sea.

Perhaps it may be the last time he will ever tread these grounds, for which he was doing so much, and I shall, in all probability, never again see the place, where, in spite of much suffering, I have also enjoyed much pleasure.

We gathered many seeds and roots, which I hope to see springing up in my own land, to remind me of this, where I have met with a kindness and hospitality never to be forgotten. . . .

On returning to the tents we found several friends assembled to take leave. The tents, indeed, had been struck, and nothing remained but the rancho, where we dined most cheerfully, though rudely enough, the servants having carried every thing but a few knives and plates on board. However, we cut forks out of pieces of wood, and passed the knives round, and, with a roast dressed in the open air, and potatoes baked in the ashes, we made our last dinner at the Herradura.

18th

Every body slept on board last night, and this morning was spent in getting in wood and water. At six o'clock, Captain Crosbie went on board the *Montezuma* to haul down Lord Cochrane's flag, and thus formally to give up the naval command in Chile.

One gun was fired, and the flag was brought on board the *Colonel Allen* to His Lordship, who was standing on the poop. He received it without apparent emotion, but desired it to be taken care of.

Some of those around him appeared more touched than he was. Under that flag he had often led them to victory, and always to honour.

Quintero is fading fast behind us, and God knows if we may any of us ever see it again. . . .

4

Brazil Journal 2

13 March – 14 June 1823

The Colonel Allen *in which they sailed was 'a dark close ship', according to Maria, and for the first few days of the voyage the weather was bad and the sea 'disagreeable'.*

On 23 January they sighted Juan Fernandez, 'the very island of Alexander Selkirk', original of Maria's favourite hero, Robinson Crusoe. They anchored the following night in bright moonlight, and for a long time stayed on deck drinking in the beauty of the place.

The following day they landed for the ship to take on water supplies. While the admiral and some of the crew energetically climbed a pinnacle to get their bearings, Maria and Glennie wandered among the ruined cottages and gardens of what had long ago been a military garrison. Here among a tangle of roses that had gone wild they found apple, pear and quince trees, cherries almost ripe, and great beds of garden mint and parsley.

They returned to find Lord Cochrane and the others sitting round a table cloth of fig leaves on which was spread a picnic, claret was cooling in a stream. Afterwards she and Lord Cochrane went botanizing together until it was time to go back to the ship.

She returned to this Paradiso the following day, and finding a seat beneath a vine began sketching, exulting at being on her own in such a magnificent wilderness. After an hour or two however she found lines from Cowper's Alexander Selkirk *running through her head:*

> Oh, solitude! where are thy charms?
> That sages have seen in thy face?
> Better dwell in the midst of alarms
> Than reign in this horrible place.

and when she saw two of her companions coming down the hill she ran thankfully to meet them.

147

They sailed from Juan Fernandez on the 28th, and after a good run doubled Cape Horn fifteen days later, finally anchoring at Rio on the 13 March.

She had been away from Brazil a year and three days.

Much had happened. For although the parliament at Lisbon had continued to legislate for Brazil 'as if it were a settlement on the coast of savage Africa', the Prince Regent, Dom Pedro, had continued to defy it, and with increasing success.

In May 1822 after a successful tour of the provinces of St Paul and Mines, the Prince had returned to his newly elected Brazilian Assembly and been awarded the flowery title of Constitutional Prince Regent and Perpetual Defender of the Kingdom of Brazil. *The same assembly had further determined that no decree from the Lisbon parliament should be implemented without his express approval.*

In June the Independence of Brazil had been openly asserted. In July a French army officer had been put in command of the considerable Brazilian army now opposed to the royalist forces holding Bahia under General Madeira, appointed from Lisbon.

In September, when the latest despatches from Lisbon arrived revoking the Prince's decrees, and demanding total submission to Portuguese rule, the Prince snatched them, threw them to the earth, and ground them underfoot.

In October he was hailed as Emperor of Brazil, in December crowned.

Yet at the beginning of 1823 Portuguese forces still held Bahia from whose harbour the Portuguese squadron continued to exercise control over the Brazilian coast. If independence was ever to become a reality for Brazil, if the new Emperor's authority was to be recognized over the whole of that former Portuguese colony, the port of Bahia must be taken.

March 13th, 1823. On board the Col. Allen, at anchor in Rio de Janeiro

One of the most windy and rainy days that I ever remember seeing in Brazil; so that the beautiful landscape of the harbour is entirely lost to the strangers from Chile, and I cannot get ashore either to provide lodgings for myself and my invalid, or to assist my friends in any way.

When the officer of the visiting boat came on board, the captain of the ship showed him into the cabin, and left him with me. I found he spoke English, and immediately began to enquire of him concerning the news of Rio. . . . Having told me so much, the officer began to question me in my turn, – Did I come from Chile? Did I know Lord Cochrane? was he coming to Rio? for all eyes were turned towards him.

When he found that His Lordship was actually on board, he flew to his cabin door, and entreated to kiss his hands, then snatched his hat, and calling to the captain to do as he would, and anchor where he pleased without ceremony, jumped over the side to be the first, if possible, to convey to the Emperor the joyful intelligence.

Nearly the same scene was acted over when Perez, the port-captain, came on board, and in a few minutes Captain Garcao of the *Liberal* came to pay his respects, and shortly afterwards Captain Taylor of the *Nitherohy*, from whom we learned something more of the state of His Imperial Majesty's fleet.

The *Pedro Primeiro*, formerly the *Martim Freitas*, had been left by the King in want of thorough repair, this she has had, and came out of dock yesterday. She is said to sail well. The *Caroline* is a fine frigate, but not commissioned, for want of men. The *Unao* is a very fine ship, wants copper, and is commanded by Captain Jewitt. The *Nitherohy* is a corvette, well found, and in good repair, but a heavy sailer, and the *Maria da Gloria*, a fine corvette, is commanded by a French officer, Captain Beaurepair.

The great difficulty the navy here has to dread is the want of men. Portuguese sailors are worse than none; few Brazilians are sailors at all, and French, English, and Americans are very scarce. The Emperor is fond of the navy, and very active in looking into every department. . . .

The weather cleared up in the afternoon, and I went ashore to see if I could find any of my old friends, or hear any news. But all the English were gone to their country-houses, and the opera, the proper place for gossip, is shut, because it is Lent. So I returned to the brig, and found Lord Cochrane ready to go ashore to wait on the Emperor, who had come in from San Cristovao to meet him at the palace in town.

His Lordship and Captain Crosbie, who went with him, did not return till late, but then well pleased with their reception.

March 14th

Another day of such heavy rain, that I have no chance of landing my invalid. Mr May came on board, and told me I might have Sir T. Hardy's* house for a few days, till I can get one for myself. He also gives us good accounts of the government, its finances, &c.

---

* Admiral Sir Thomas Masterman Hardy (1769–1839). Fought at Trafalgar with Nelson. Commander-in-Chief Southern American Squadron.

An embargo has been laid on all vessels to-day, to prevent the news of Lord Cochrane's arrival from reaching Bahia.

15th

I went early ashore to prepare for leaving the brig. I observed two of the arches, under which the Emperor had passed on the day of coronation, designed in extremely good taste, and well executed. They are of course only temporary. Some more solid works have been executed, since I last saw Rio, new fountains opened, aqueducts repaired, all the forts and other public works visibly improved, and the streets new paved. There is besides every where an air of business.

I carried Glennie ashore in the afternoon, and was foolish enough to feel very sorry to leave my fellow-passengers, and still more foolish to be vexed at the perfect indifference with which they saw me go. Both perhaps natural enough. I am once more without any one to lean to, and alone in the world with my melancholy charge. They have business and pleasure before them.

It was a fine evening, and the little voyage in the boat to Botafogo seemed to do Glennie good, but we had the mortification to find that neither the provisions I had bought in the town had arrived, nor the servant one of my friends had promised to procure me. So we were alone and supperless, but, thank God, not helpless.

I have learned so much in my wanderings as not to be dependent, and so, after a time, I had from the huckster's shop in the neighbourhood a tolerable *tea* to give my invalid, and sent him to bed in pretty good spirits, and took time afterwards to be pretty miserable myself.

March 20th

These past days I have employed in looking about for a house, and have succeeded, in receiving and returning the visits of my old acquaintance, and in being very unwell.

I hear there is nothing yet settled about Lord Cochrane's command. The world says that he was asked to serve under two Portuguese admirals and for Portuguese pay. Of course, these are terms he could never accept. I have not seen him, so am not sure about this. I suppose, however, it is true, or he would not still be living on board that dirty little brig in which we arrived.

21st

Whatever difficulties were in the way of Lord Cochrane's command, they are over. I have a note from him announcing that he hoists his flag at four o'clock this afternoon, on board the *Pedro Primeiro*.

22d

Captain Bourchier of His Majesty's ship *Beaver* kindly lent me his boat to-day, to convey me with my cousin and my goods to my cottage on the Gloria hill, close to Mr May's, and not very far from the house the government has given as a temporary residence to Lord Cochrane.

It is pleasant to me on many accounts, it is cool, and there is a shady walk for the sick. It is almost surrounded by the sea, which breaks against the wall, and not being near any road, we shall be perfectly quiet here.

Friday, 28th

This has been a busy week, both to me and to my friends, who are hurrying every thing to get to sea as quickly as possible, as it is of the utmost consequence to free Bahia of the enemy.

Saturday, 29th

His Majesty's ship *Tartar*, Captain Brown, arrived to-day from England, bringing no good news of any kind.

In the first place, Lord Cochrane suffers extreme distress on learning that Lady Cochrane and her infant daughter are on their way to Chile, so that they will have to perform the rough passage round Cape Horn twice before he sees them, and in the next, Captain Brown gives a most formidable account of a Portuguese fleet bound for Bahia, which he met on this side of the line.

I trust he is mistaken in the last, and I try to comfort Lord Cochrane as to the first piece of intelligence, by suggestions, of the probability, if not certainty, that the ship Lady Cochrane will sail in, must touch in this port. However, his natural anxiety is not to be overcome.

Monday, March 31st

Yesterday the *Pedro Primeiro* dropped down the harbour, as far as Boa Viage, and to-day I went with Lord Cochrane on board of her.

We found that the Emperor and Empress had been on board at day-light. On some of the Portuguese officers complaining that the English sailors had been drunk the day before, the Empress said, 'Oh, 'tis the custom of the North, where brave men come from. The sailors are under my protection; I spread my mantle over them.'

The *Pedro Primeiro* is a fine two-decker, without a poop. She has a most beautiful gun-deck, but I could not see her to advantage, as she was still taking in stores, and receiving men.

Her cabins are beautifully fitted up with handsome wood and green morocco cushions, &c., and I am told the Emperor takes great pride in her. Captain Crosbie commands her; and three lieutenants who came with us from Chile are appointed to her. . . .

10th [April]

Nothing of any note or variety has taken place during these ten days. Glennie is gaining ground, I write and read, and attend to him.

The *Nitherohy* sails to-morrow to join Lord Cochrane off Bahia, with three mortars on board, two 10, and one 13-inch. I find, with surprise, that the cartridges are still made up here in canvass, not flannel, and I fear that the ships are not so well found as I wish them, great part of the canvass and cordage have been seventeen years in store, and, I should fear, partly rotten.

But all this is nothing to the evil attending the having Portuguese among the crews. 'Tis not natural they should fight against their countrymen.

I have had the pleasure of reading *Peveril of the Peak** within these few days. 'Tis a sort of historical portrait, like *Kenilworth*, where the Duke of Buckingham, he who

> In one revolving moon
> Was hero, fiddler, statesman, and buffoon,

is the principal figure. Charles II and the rest of the court serve for the black boy and parrot in costume, while the story of *Peveril* is nothing more than the carved-work frieze of the very pleasant apartment he has been placed in.

---

* By Sir Walter Scott.

14th

The *Fly* sloop of war, and the packet from England, came in and brought the news of the war between France and Spain.* This news is, of course, interesting here, as Portugal is considered to be implicated in the disputes in Europe. And then, the part England may take, and how that may affect this country, is a subject of anxious speculation. . . .

15th

Glennie has been gaining so much strength lately, that he has determined on joining the Commodore at Bahia, and this day he left me, to sail in His Majesty's ship *Beaver*.

After having had him to attend to for six months, and being used to constant intercourse with an intelligent inmate, I feel so very lonely, that I believe I must leave off some of my sedentary habits, and visit a little among my neighbours. . . .

May 1st

I have this day seen the Val Longo. It is the slave-market of Rio. Almost every house in this very long street is a depot for slaves.

On passing by the doors this evening, I saw in most of them long benches placed near the walls, on which rows of young creatures were sitting, their heads shaved, their bodies emaciated, and the marks of recent itch upon their skins. In some places the poor creatures were lying on mats, evidently too sick to sit up.

At one house the half-doors were shut, and a group of boys and girls, apparently not above fifteen years old, and some much under, were leaning over the hatches, and gazing into the street with wondering faces. They were evidently quite new negroes.

As I approached them, it appears that something about me attracted their attention. They touched one another, to be sure that all saw me, and then chattered in their own African dialect with great eagerness. I went and stood near them, and though certainly more disposed to weep, I forced myself to smile to them, and look cheerfully, and kissed my hand to them, with all which they seemed delighted, and jumped about and danced, as if returning my civilities.

Poor things! I would not, if I could, shorten their moments of

* The French, as agents of the Holy Alliance Congress, had invaded Spain to suppress the newly won rights of the Spanish constitutionalists.

glee, by awakening them to a sense of the sad things of slavery, but, if I could, I would appeal to their masters, to those who buy, and to those who sell, and implore them to think of the evils slavery brings, not only to the negroes but to themselves. Not only to themselves but to their families and their posterity. . . .

I have hitherto endeavoured, without success, to procure a correct statement of the number of slaves imported into all Brazil. I fear, indeed, it will be hardly possible for me to do so, on account of the distance of some of the ports, but I will not rest till I procure at least a statement of the number entered at the custom-house here during the last two years.*

The number of ships from Africa that I see constantly entering the harbour, and the multitudes that throng the slave-houses in this street, convince me that the importation must be very great. The ordinary proportion of deaths on the passage is, I am told, about one in five.

May 3d

Early this morning the French naval captain, La Susse, called on me to take me in his boat to town, for the purpose of going to Señhor Luis José's house in the Rua do Ouvidor, to see the Emperor go in state to the opening of the Constituent and Legislative Assembly. All the great officers of state, all the gentlemen of the household, most of the nobility, and several regiments accompanied him. . . .

The carriages displayed to-day would form a curious collection for a museum in London or Paris. Some were the indescribable sort of caleche used here, and in the middle of these was a very gay pea-green and silver chariot, evidently built in Europe, very light, with silver ornaments, silver fellies to the wheels, silver where any kind of metal could be used, and beautiful embossed silver plates on the harness of the mules.

Many other gala carriages seemed as if they had been built in the age of Louis xiv. Such things! mounted on horizontal leathern bands, and all other kind of savage hangings, besides paint and gilding, and, by-the-bye, some very handsome silver and silver gilt harnesses. Then there were splendid liveries, and all manner of gaudiness, not without some taste.

The houses were hung with all the damask and satin of every

---

* She later obtained two statements of custom-house entries at Rio, 21,199 slaves imported in 1821, 24,934 in 1822.

colour that they could supply; and the balconies stored with ladies, whose bright eyes rain influence, dressed in gala dresses, with feathers and diamonds in profusion; and as the royal carriages passed, we waved our handkerchiefs, and scattered flowers on their heads. . . .

May 12th

I have been too unwell to do any thing, and only write to-day to notice the arrival of the *Jupiter* frigate, with Lord Amherst* on his way to India, and the rumour that he has some official character at this court. . . .

16th

. . . The *Doris* is arrived from Bahia. She has had no direct communication with Lord Cochrane's little squadron; but it seems, that with his six ships, he keeps the enemy's fleet of fifteen sail in check. The town of Bahia is said to be in a dreadful state for want of provisions. The slaves are daily dying in the streets. Some houses, after appearing shut up for some days, have been opened by the police officers, who have found the masters escaped, and the slaves dead. . . . The little fresh provision that finds its way into the town is exorbitantly dear. General Madeira has proclaimed martial-law in the place, he has seized some corn and flour out of a neutral ship, and has raised forced loans from all classes, both native and foreign . . .

We are becoming very anxious indeed for news from His Lordship: many rumours are afloat; but as there has been no direct communication from the squadron, they only increase the general anxiety.

May 17th

Soon after I arrived here, in March, or rather as soon as my patient Glennie left me, I felt that, as a stranger here, and situated as I am, I was particularly unprotected, and therefore I spoke to the minister José Bonifacio, telling him my feelings; and saying, that from the amiable character of the Empress, I should wish to be allowed to wait on her, and to consider her as protecting me while I remain in

---

* William Pitt, Earl Amherst (1773–1857), governor general of India.

the empire. She accordingly promised to fix a day for me to see her, but a severe indisposition has hitherto confined her to her room.

Now, Lady Amherst having requested to see Her Imperial Majesty, the day after to-morrow is fixed on for the purpose, and I have an intimation that I shall be received on the same day, as the Empress wishes not to receive any other foreigner before me. This is polite, or rather it is more, it is really kind.

19th

Though I was suffering exceedingly this morning, I resolved nevertheless to attend the Empress at noon, at San Cristovaŏ. I was obliged to take a quantity of opium, to enable me to do so.

However, I arrived at the appointed time, and, as I had been desired to do, asked for the *camarista môr*, José Bonifacio's sister, and was shown into the presence-chamber, where I found that lady and Lady Amherst, Miss Amherst, and Mrs Chamberlain.

The Empress entered shortly after, in a handsome morning dress of purple satin, with white ornaments, and looking extremely well. Mrs Chamberlain presented Lady and Miss Amherst, and Her Imperial Majesty spoke for some minutes with Her Ladyship. After which she motioned to me to go to her, which I did.

She spoke to me most kindly; and said, in a very flattering way, that she had long known me by name, and several other things that persons in her rank can make so agreeable by voice and manner, and I left her with the most agreeable impressions. She is extremely like several persons whom I have seen of the Austrian Imperial family,* and has a remarkably sweet expression. . . .

Saturday, June 7th

Since the day I was at San Cristovaŏ, I have been confined to my room, and totally unable to exert myself, either mind or body, from severe indisposition.

The *Creole* is come in from Bahia, to get provisions, preparatory to going home. The Commodore has offered me a passage in her, and has written to that purpose, but I am in no state to embark for a long voyage.

The accounts from Bahia are sadder than ever. As to the Bahians, though favourable to the Imperial† cause the misery of the poor inhabitants is great indeed.

* She had been the Archduchess Maria Leopoldina.
† That is, the Brazilian cause.

12th

We have been for three days kept in a state of agitation by reports that Bahia has fallen, and various rumours attending those reports. They all turn out to have arisen from a *russe de guerre* of Madeira, who contrived to despatch a small vessel to a port on the coast for flour, pretending that it was for Lord Cochrane, and spreading that report to cover its real purpose.

13th

A brig, prize to the squadron, arrived, and also the *Sesostris*, a merchant ship bound to Valparaiso, on board of which were Lady Cochrane and her family going to Chile.

Thank God, by putting in here, she has learned where Lord Cochrane is, and is thus spared the tedious voyage, and her excellent husband much anxiety on her account.

14th

At length we have true news both from and of Lord Cochrane. I wrote to Lady Cochrane, excusing myself on account of illness from going to her, and she kindly called on me as she landed, and a few minutes afterwards I received letters from the Admiral, and from some others in the squadron. . . .

The news when she read it pleased her. In spite of rotten ship's gear, near mutinous Portuguese crews, and being outnumbered thirteen to five by the enemy, Lord Cochrane had engaged, cut the enemy in two and forced them to take refuge in Bahia. The Imperial Brazilian forces in the meantime had gained a considerable victory over the forces of General Madeira.

Lord Cochrane in the interests of having at least one ship with a dependable crew had removed English seamen and officers from two of the Brazilian vessels into his flagship, the Pedro Primeiro.

19 June – 15 August 1823

June 19th

My health grows worse and worse. The *Creole* sailed to-day. I have amused myself for two days with some English newspapers. If any thing can rouse me to health it surely ought to be news from England. . . .

I see with pleasure a virtual acknowledgment from the English ministers of the independence of Spanish America.

22d

This is the eve of St John's, whereon the maidens of Brazil practise some of the same rites as those of Scotland do at Hallowe'en, to ascertain the fate of their loves. They burn nuts together; they put their hands, blindfold, on a table, with the letters of the alphabet, and practise many a simple conjuration.

I think I recollect long ago to have seen the maid-servants of a house in Berkshire place an herb, I think a kind of stone-crop, behind the door, calling it Midsummer men, that was to chain the favoured youth as he entered.

For me I only wish for the *nucca* drop of the Arab to fall this night, so I might catch it, and be relieved from my weary sickness.

June 26th

My friend, Dr Dickson, who has attended me all this time with unvarying kindness, having advised change of air for me, he and Mr May have pitched on a small house on Botafogo beach, having an upper story, which is considered as an advantage here, the ground-floor houses being often a little damp. To-day Captain Willis of the *Brazen* brought me in his boat to my new dwelling. . . .

July 1st

A good deal of sensation has been excited to-day of rather a painful nature. The Emperor has fallen from his horse, and has broken two of his ribs, and is otherwise much bruised. However, his youth and strength prevent any serious apprehension from the consequences of his accident.

There is no public news, and I am much too ill to care for any other. A foreigner, and alone, and very sick, I have abundant leisure to see the worth to the world of riches, or the appearance of them, and show and parade, and to feel that if I had them all, they could neither relieve the head nor the heart of the suffering or the sorrowful.

I think I am grown selfish. I cannot interest myself in the little things of other people's lives as I used to do. I require the strong stimulus of public interest to rouse my attention. . . .

Just such a stimulus arrived sixteen days later and with tonic effect:

> My dear Madam [*wrote Lord Cochrane*],
> I have been grieved to learn your indisposition, but you must recover now that I tell you we have starved the enemy out of Bahia. The forts were abandoned this morning, and the men of war, 13 in number, with about 32 sail of transports and merchant vessels, are under sail. We shall follow (*i.e. the* Maria da Gloria *and* Pedro Primeiro) *to the* world's end. I say again expect good news. Ever believe me your sincere and respectful friend,
> > Cochrane
> 2d July, 1823.
> Eight miles north of Bahia.[1]

July 23d

I had for some time promised to paint a sketch of San Cristavaŏ* for the Empress, and to-day I resolved to carry it to her. So I went, and on my way breakfasted at my good friend the Viscondeca do Rio Seco's. I then proceeded to the palace, and went up first to enquire after the Emperor's health. While I was writing my name, he, having perceived me arrive from the window, politely sent to say he would see me, and accordingly I was ushered into the presence-chamber by the Viador Don Luiz da Ponte. There I saw ministers and generals all in state.

The Emperor was in a small inner room, where were his piano, his shooting apparatus, &c. He was in an undressed cotton jacket with his arm in a sling, but looking well, although thinner and paler than formerly.

He sent for the little picture, with which he seemed much

---

* The Imperial Palace.

pleased, and after speaking for some time very politely in French, I made my courtesy and retired.

I then went to the Empress's apartment. She was out, but I was asked to wait for her return from her walk, and in the meantime I saw the young Princesses, who are extremely fair, and like Her Imperial Majesty, especially the eldest, Doña Maria da Gloria, who has one of the most intelligent faces I have seen.

The Empress came in soon, and talked to me a good while on a variety of subjects, and very kindly of my late illness.

Setting aside the consideration of her high rank, it is not a little pleasing to me to meet so well-educated and well-bred a woman, and I felt quite sorry to leave her without telling her so. She is in all respects an amiable and respectable woman. No distressed person ever applies to her in vain; and her conduct, both public and private, justly commands the admiration and love of her family and subjects. . . .

July 25th

Our society at Botafogo is enlivened by the arrival of Commodore Sir T. Hardy, who occupies the house of the disembargador França, and who is not only cheerful and sociable himself, but causes cheerfulness around him.

The officers of his own ship, and those of the rest of the squadron, are of course great acquisitions to the parties at Rio, but I see little of them, my dull house, and duller self, offering nothing inviting except to the midshipmen of my old ship, who visit me very constantly.

I have bought a small horse for the sake of exercise, and sometimes accompany the boys on their evening rides. . . .

August 3d

I drank tea at the Baronesa de Campos', and met a large family party, which always assembles on Sundays to pay their respects to the old lady. The tea was made by one of the young ladies, with the assistance of her sister, just as it would be in England.

A large silver urn, silver tea-pots, milk-jugs, and sugar-dishes, with elegant china, were placed on a large table round which several of the young people assembled, and sent round the tea to us, who sat at a distance. All sorts of bread, cakes, buttered toast, and rusks were handed with the tea; and after it was removed, sweetmeats of every description were presented, after which every body took a glass of water.

6th

Sailed to-day, HM ship *Beaver*, with my friend Mr Dance as acting captain.

The world says she takes some very important despatches relating to the commerce of England with the independent provinces of La Plata, but as the world often tells what is not true, and as what is true is never confessed by those who know officially, I never trouble myself to ask about these things.

I am sorry to see almost my last friend leave the station before me, but I am now so used to losing, one way or another, all who from any motive have ever acted or felt kindly to me, that I hope soon to grow callous to the pain such loss still gives.

It is in vain that I flatter myself that I have recovered the tone of my mind. I am affected even to weakness by every little incident, and am obliged to take refuge from my private feelings, in the interest that I have lately forced myself to take in the affairs of this country. Surely, where the happiness of millions of its fellow-creatures is at stake, the human heart may unblamed busy itself. . . .

12th

This day, as well as yesterday and the day before, there have been illuminations and dressed operas on account of the Emperor's recovery. To-night a vessel, prize to the squadron, arrived, bringing news of their wellbeing, and of the arrival of many prizes at Bahia and Pernambuco.

As officers and men from the Imperial ships cannot be spared in sufficient numbers to work the prizes into port, Lord Cochrane makes sure of their going thither by starting the water, excepting what is sufficient for a certain number of days, and cutting away the main and mizen masts, so that they must run for the ports to leeward. Seamen will appreciate this. . . .

August 15th

. . . I went in the evening to a ball and concert at the Baronesa de Campos'. On entering, I was met by the young ladies of the family, and led up to their grandmother, and after paying my compliments to her, I was placed among the division of the family where I had most acquaintance.

There were only two Englishwomen besides Lady Cochrane and myself, and these were the wives of the consul and the commissioner for the slave business. A foreign gentleman present remarked, that though we were but four, we hardly conversed together.* This was perfectly true. I like, when I am in foreign society, to talk to foreigners, and think it neither wise nor civil to form coteries with those of one's own nation in such cases. . . .

After the first dance was over, we walked all about the house, and found a magnificent dining-room as to size, but scarcely furnished to correspond with the rest of the house. The bed-rooms and dressing-rooms of the ladies are neat and elegantly fitted up with English and French furniture, and all as different as possible from the houses I saw in Bahia.

I am told that they are likewise as different from what they were here twenty years since, and can well believe it. Even during the twelve months of my absence from Rio, I see a wonderful polishing has taken place, and every thing is gaining an European air.

I took the liberty of remarking to one of the ladies, the extreme youth of some of the children who accompanied their mothers this evening, and saying, that in England we should consider it injurious to them in all respects.

She asked me what we did with them. I told her that some of them would be in bed, and others with their nurses and governesses. She said we were happy in that, but that here, there were no such persons, and that the children would be left to the care and example of the slaves, whose manners were so depraved, and practices so immoral, that it must be the destruction of the children. Those who loved their children must keep them under their own eyes, where, if they were brought too forward in company, they at least could learn no ill.

I love to collect these proofs of the evils of slavery – even here where it exists in a milder form than in most countries. . . .

Meantime, having long wanted to see more of the country surrounding Rio, she determined on an expedition to Vera Cruz some fifty miles off, taking a black servant as an escort. But as always, there was a young man at hand eager to escort her. This time it was Mr Dampier, young, well-bred and intelligent, who also shared with Maria a love for the picturesque.

They set out on 20 August, he on a large raw-boned horse and decked out

---

* Also, Maria had a poor opinion of Lady Cochrane.

in short jacket, huge straw hat and a brace of pistols round his waist; she on a little grey horse, wearing her grey habit and sporting a smaller straw hat. Accompanying them was Antonio, 'the merriest of negroes', on a mule. . . .

29 August – 18 December 1823

August 29th

To-day I received a visit from Doña Maria de Jesus, the young woman who has lately distinguished herself in the war of the Reconcave. Her dress is that of a soldier of one of the Emperor's battalions, with the addition of a tartan kilt, which she told me she had adopted from a picture representing a highlander, as the most feminine military dress. What would the Gordons and MacDonalds say to this? The 'garb of old Gaul', chosen as a womanish attire!

Her father is a Portuguese, named Gonsalvez de Almeida, and possesses a farm on the Rio do Pex, in the parish of San José, in the Certaŏ, about forty leagues inland from Cachoeira. Her mother was also a Portuguese; yet the young woman's features, especially her eyes and forehead, have the strongest characteristics of the Indians. . . .

Doña Maria told me several particulars concerning the country, and more concerning her own adventures. It appears, that early in the late war of the Reconcave, emissaries had traversed the country in all directions, to raise patriot recruits, that one of these had arrived at her father's house one day about dinner time, that her father had invited him in, and that after their meal he began to talk on the subject of his visit.

He represented the greatness and the riches of Brazil, and the happiness to which it might attain if independent. He set forth the long and oppressive tyranny of Portugal, and the meanness of submitting to be ruled by so poor and degraded a country. He talked long and eloquently of the services Don Pedro had rendered to Brazil, of his virtues, and those of the Empress, so that at the last, said the girl,

'I felt my heart burning in my breast.'

Her father, however, had none of her enthusiasm of character. He is old, and said he neither could join the army himself, nor had he a son to send thither, and as to giving a slave for the ranks, what interest had a slave to fight for the independence of Brazil? He should wait in patience the result of the war, and be a peaceable subject to the winner.

Doña Maria stole from home to the house of her own sister, who was married, and lived at a little distance. She recapitulated the whole of the stranger's discourse, and said she wished she was a man, that she might join the patriots.

'Nay,' said the sister, 'if I had not a husband and children, for one half of what you say I would join the ranks for the Emperor.'

This was enough. Maria received some clothes belonging to her sister's husband to equip her, and as her father was then about to go to Cachoeira to dispose of some cottons, she resolved to take the opportunity of riding after him, near enough for protection in case of accident on the road, and far enough off to escape detection.

At length being in sight of Cachoeira, she stopped, and going off the road, equipped herself in male attire, and entered the town.

This was on Friday. By Sunday she had managed matters so well, that she had entered the regiment of artillery, and had mounted guard. She was too slight, however, for that service, and exchanged into the infantry, where she now is.

She was sent hither, I believe, with despatches, and to be presented to the Emperor, who has given her an ensign's commission and the order of the cross, the decoration of which he himself fixed on her jacket.

She is illiterate, but clever. Her understanding is quick, and her perceptions keen. I think, with education she might have been a remarkable person. She is not particularly masculine in her appearance, and her manners are gentle and cheerful. She has not contracted any thing coarse or vulgar in her camp life, and I believe that no imputation has ever been substantiated against her modesty. One thing is certain, that her sex never was known until her father applied to her commanding officer to seek her.

There is nothing very peculiar in her manners at table, excepting that she eats farinha* with her eggs at breakfast and her fish at dinner, instead of bread, and smokes a segar after each meal, but she is very temperate. . . .

September 14th

I observed on the beach to-day a line of red sandy-looking matter, extending all along the shore, and tinging the sea for several feet from the edge. At night this red edge became luminous, and I now recollect when on the passage to India in 1809, that on observing a peculiar luminous appearance of the sea, we took up a bucket of

* Meal.

water, and on examining it next morning, we observed a similar red grainy substance floating in it. It is the first time I have seen it here, and I cannot find that any body has paid any attention to it.

Perhaps it is not worth noticing, but I am so much alone, that I have grown more and more alive to all the appearances of inanimate nature. Besides, I must make much of the country, as in a few days I have to take up my abode in one of the narrow close streets of Rio, and this not from choice.

It is the custom here, and a very natural and pleasant one it is, for every family that can, to live in the country all the summer, so that the houses of every kind, in the country, are in great request. The term for that which I live in was hired is expired, and I am therefore obliged to leave it.

My going to town, perhaps, might be avoided, but there are some things I shall probably learn more perfectly by living there, and, besides, does not Lord Bacon advise that in order to profit much from travel, one should not only move from city to city, 'but change his lodgings from one end and part of the city to another?' . . .

18th

I went to-day to the public library to ask about some books, and am invited to go and use what I like there. The librarians are all extremely polite, and the library is open to all persons for six hours daily. . . .

23d

I have been unwell again – but I find that staying at home does not cure me. So I went both yesterday and to-day to the library, where a pleasant, cool, little cabinet has been assigned to me, where whatever book I ask for is brought to me, and where I have pen, ink, and paper always placed to make notes. This is a kindness and attention to a woman and a stranger that I was hardly prepared for. . . .

I have begun to read diligently every scrap of Brazilian history I can find, and I have commenced by a collection of pamphlets, newspapers, some MS. letters and proclamations, from the year 1576 to 1757, bound up together.

Some of these tracts Mr Southey* mentions, others he probably

---

* Robert Southey (1774–1843), *History of Brazil (1810–19)*.

had not seen, but they contain nothing very material that he has not in his history.

This morning's study of Brazilian history in the original language is one great advantage I derive from my removal into town. Besides which, I speak now less English than Portuguese. . . .

Let no one say, that he is too miserable for any comfort to reach him. My health weak, my nerves irritable, and having neither wealth nor rank. Forced to receive obligations painful and discordant with my former habits and prejudices, and often meeting with impertinence from those who take advantage of my solitary situation. But I am nevertheless sure that I have more *half-hours*, (I dare not say *hours*,) of true enjoyment, and fewer days of real misery, than half of those whom the world accounts happy.

And I thank God, who gave me the temper to feel grief exquisitely, that he at the same time gave me an equal capacity for joy. And it is a joy to find minds that can understand and communicate with our own, to meet occasionally with persons of similar habits of thinking, and who, when the business of life rests a while, seek recreation in the same pursuits. This delight I do oftener enjoy than I could have hoped, so far from cultivated Europe.

One or two of my friends are, indeed, like costly jewels, not to be worn every day, but there are several of sterling metal that even here disarm the ills of this 'working-day world' of half their sting. . . .

30th

I called at a very agreeable Brazilian lady's house to-day; and saw, for the first time in my life, a regular Brazilian *bas-blue* in the person of Doña Maria Clara. She reads a good deal, especially philosophy and politics. She is a tolerable botanist, and draws flowers exceedingly well. Besides, she is what I think it is Miss Edgeworth calls 'a fetcher and carrier of bays' – a useful member of society, who, without harming herself or others, circulates the necessary literary news, and would be invaluable where new authors want puffing, and new poems should have the pretty passages pointed out for the advantage of literary misses.

Here, alas! such kindly offices are confined to comparing the rival passages in the *Correiro* and the *Sentinella*, or advocating the cause of the editor of the *Sylpho* or the *Tamoyo*. But, in sober earnest, I was delighted to find such a lady.

Without arrogating much more than is due to the sex, it may claim some small influence over the occupations and amusements of home. And the woman who brings books instead of cards or private scandal into the domestic circle, is likely to promote a more general cultivation, and a more refined taste, in the society to which she belongs.

October 1st, 1823

The court and city are in a state of rejoicing. Lord Cochrane has secured Maranham* for the Emperor. Once more I break in on my own rule, and copy part of his letter to me:

Maranham, August 12th, 1823.

My dear Madam,

You would receive a few lines from me, dated from off Bahia, and also from the latitude of Pernambuco, saying briefly what we were about then. And now I have to add, that we followed the Portuguese squadron to the fifth degree of north latitude, and until only thirteen sail remained together out of seventy of their convoy; and then, judging it better for the interests of His Imperial Majesty, I hauled the wind for Maranham; and I have the pleasure to tell you, that my plan of adding it to the empire has had complete success. I ran in with this ship abreast of their forts, and having sent a notice of blockade, and intimated that the squadron of Bahia and Imperial forces were off the bar, the Portuguese flag was hauled down, and every thing went on without bloodshed, just as you could wish.

We have found here a Portuguese brig of war, a schooner, and eight gun-boats, also sixteen merchant vessels, and a good deal of property belonging to Portuguese resident in Lisbon, deposited in the custom-house.

The brig of war late the Infante Don Miguel, *now the* Maranham, *is gone down with Grenfell to summon Para, where there is a beautiful newly-launched fifty-gun frigate, which I have no doubt but he has got before now.*

Thus, my dear Madam, on my return I shall have the pleasure to acquaint His Imperial Majesty, that between the extremities of his empire there exists no enemy either on shore or afloat. This will probably be within the sixth month from our sailing from Rio, and at this moment is actually the case.

9th

I resolved to take a holiday: so went to spend it with Mrs May, at

* On the coast of north-eastern Brazil.

the Gloria, only going first for half an hour to the library.

That library is a great source of comfort to me, I every day find my cabinet quiet and cool, and provided with the means of study, and generally spend four hours there, reading Portuguese and Brazilian history, for which I shall not, probably, have so good an opportunity again. . . .

October 12th

This is the Emperor's birth-day, and the first anniversary of the coronation.

I was curious to see the court of Brazil, so I rose early and dressed myself, and went to the royal chapel, where the Emperor and Empress, and the Imperial Princess were to be with the court before the drawing-room.

I accordingly applied to the chaplain for a station, who showed me into what is called the *diplomatic* tribune, but it is in fact for respectable foreigners, there I met all manner of consuls.

However, the curiosity which led me to the chapel would not allow me to go home when the said consuls did, so I went to the drawing-room, which, perhaps, after all, I should not have done, being quite alone, had not the gracious manner in which their Imperial Majesties saluted me, both in the chapel and afterwards in the corridor leading to the royal apartments, induced me to proceed.

I reached the inner room where the ladies were, just as the Emperor had, with a most pleasing compliment, announced to Lady Cochrane that she was Marchioness of Maranhan, for that he had made her husband Marques, and had conferred on him the highest degree of the order of the Cruceiro.

I am sometimes absent, and now, when I ought to have been most attentive, I felt myself in the situation Sancho Panca so humorously describes, of sending my wits wool-gathering, and coming home shorn myself. For I was so intent on the honour conferred on my friend and countryman, so charmed, that for once his services had been appreciated, that when I found the Emperor in the middle of the room, and that his hand was extended towards me, and that all others had paid their compliments and passed to their places, I forgot I had my glove on. Took his Imperial hand with that glove, and I suppose kissed it much in earnest, for I saw some of the ladies smile before I remembered any thing about it.

Had this happened with regard to any other prince, I believe that I should have run away, but nobody is more good-natured than

Don Pedro. I saw there was no harm done, and so determining to be on my guard when the Empress came in, and then to take an opportunity of telling her of my fault, I stayed quietly, and began talking to two or three young ladies who were at court for the first time, and had just received their appointment as ladies of honour to the Empress.

Her Majesty, who had retired with the young Princess, now came in, and the ladies all paid their compliments while the Emperor was busy in the presence-chamber receiving the compliments of the Assembly and other public bodies. There was little form and no stiffness. . . . It was curious, but it pleased me, to see some negro officers take the small white hand of the Empress in their clumsy black hands, and apply their pouting African lips to so delicate a skin. But they looked up to *Nosso Emperador*, and to her, with a reverence that seemed to me a promise of faith *from* them, a bond of kindness *to* them.

The Emperor was dressed in a very rich military uniform, the Empress in a white dress embroidered with gold, a corresponding cap with feathers tipped with green. Her diamonds were superb, her head-tire and ear-rings having in them opals such as I suppose the world does not contain, and the brilliants surrounding the Emperor's picture, which she wears, the largest I have seen. . . .

When their Imperial Majesties came out of the great room, I saw Madame do Rio Seco in earnest conversation with them, and soon I saw her and Lady Cochrane kissing hands, and found they had both been appointed honorary ladies of the Empress. Then the Viscountess told me she had been speaking to the Empress about me.

This astonished me, for I had no thought of engaging in any thing away from England. Six months before, indeed, I had said that I was so pleased with the little Princess, that I should like to educate her. . . . I said, that if the Emperor and Empress chose (as a warm climate agreed with me), I should not dislike it, that it required consideration, and that if I could render myself sufficiently agreeable to the Empress, I should ask the appointment of governess to the Princess. . . .

I own that the more I saw of the Imperial family, the more I wished to belong to it. But I was frightened at the thoughts of Rio, by the impertinent behaviour of some of the English, so that I should probably not have proposed the thing myself.

It was done, however, the Empress told me to apply to the Emperor. I observed he looked tired with the levee, and begged to be allowed to write to her another day.

She said, 'Write if you please, but come and see the Emperor at five o'clock to-morrow.' And so they went out, and I remained marvelling at the chance that had brought me into a situation so unlike any thing I had ever contemplated, and came home to write a letter to Her Imperial Majesty, and to wonder what I should do next.

Monday, October 13th

I wrote my letter to the Empress, and was punctual to the time for seeing the Emperor. He received me very kindly, and sent me to speak to Her Imperial Majesty, who took my letter, and promised me an answer in two days, adding the most obliging expressions of personal kindness. And this was certainly the first letter I ever wrote on the subject, though my English *friends* tell me that I had a memorial in my hand yesterday, and that I went to court only to deliver it, for they saw it in my hand.

Now I had a white pocket-handkerchief and a black fan in my hand, and thought as little of speaking about my own affairs to their Imperial Majesties, as of making a voyage to the moon. But people will always know each other's affairs best.

16th

I have continued going regularly to the library, and have become acquainted with the principal librarian, who is also the Emperor's confessor. . . . To-day, on returning from my study I received a letter from the Empress, written in English, full of kind expressions, and in the pleasantest manner accepting, in the Emperor's name and her own, my services as governess to her daughter, and giving me leave to go to England, before I entered on my employment, as the Princess is still so young.

I went to San Cristovaõ to return thanks.

19th

I saw the Empress, who is pleased to allow me to sail for England in the packet, the day after to-morrow. I confess I am sorry to go before Lord Cochrane's return. I had set my heart on seeing my best friend in this country, after his exertions and triumph. But I have now put my hand to the plough, and I must not turn back.

October 21st

I embarked on board the packet for England. Mrs May walked to the shore with me. Sir Murray Maxwell lent me his boats to bring myself and goods on board. I had previously taken leave of every body I knew, English and foreign. . . .

Oct. 25th

Happily for me there are no passengers in the packet, and still more happily, the captain's wife and daughter are on board, so that I feel as if lodging in a quiet English family, all is so decent, orderly, and, above all, clean.

I am under no restraint, but walk, read, write, and draw, as if at home. Every body, even to the monkey on board, looks kindly at me, and I receive all manner of friendly attention consistent with perfect liberty.

Nov. 1st

'The longest way about is often the nearest way home,' says the proverb, and, on that principle, ships bound for England from Brazil at this time of the year stand far to the eastward. We are still in the latitude of Rio de Janeiro, though in long. 29° W., and shall probably stand still nearer to the coast of Africa, before we shall be able to look to the northward. . . .

17th Lat. 5° N., long. 25° W. . . .

We spoke to the *Pambinha*, sixty days from Maranham. She says Lord Cochrane had gone himself to Para, whence he meant to proceed directly for Rio, so that he would probably be there by this time, as the *Pedro Primeiro* sails well. I had no opportunity of learning more, as the vessel passed hastily.

We have, generally speaking, had hot winds from Africa, and there is a sultry feel in the air which the state of the thermometer hardly accounts for.

I perceive that the sails are all tinged with a reddish colour; and wherever a rope has chafed upon them, they appear almost as if iron-moulded. This the captain and officers attribute to the wind from Africa.

They were certainly perfectly white long after we left Rio. They have not been either furled or unbent. What may be the nature of the dust or sand that thus on the wings of the wind crosses so many miles of ocean, and stains the canvass? Can it be this minute dust affecting the lungs which makes us breathe as if in the sultry hours preceding a thunder-storm? . . .

December 18th

After passing the Azores, a long succession of gales from the north-east kept us off the land. These were succeeded by three fine days, and the sea, which had been heavy, became smooth.

Early the day before yesterday, however, it began to blow very hard from the north-west, and yesterday morning it changed to a gale from the south and south-west, and we lay-to under storm stay-sails, in a tremendous sea.

About one o'clock the captain called to me, and desired me to come on deck and see what could not last ten minutes, and I might never see again.

I ran up, as did Mrs and Miss K—. A sudden shift of wind had taken place. We saw it before it came up, driving the sea along furiously before it, and the meeting of the two winds broke the sea as high as any ship's mast-head in a long line, like the breakers on a reef of rocks.

It was the most beautiful yet fearful sight I ever beheld, and the sea was surging over our little vessel so as to threaten to fill her, but the hatches were battoned down. We were lying-to on a right tack, and a hawser had been passed round the bits in order to sustain the foremast, in case we lost our bowsprit, as we expected to do every instant.

But in twenty minutes the gale moderated, and we bore up for Falmouth, which we reached this morning, having passed the cabin deck of a ship that doubtless had foundered in the storm of yesterday.

Once more I am in England; and, to use the words of a venerable though apocryphal writer,

Here will I make an end. And if I have done well, and as is fitting the story, it is that which I desired; but if slenderly and meanly, it is that which I could attain unto.*

M.G.

* 2 Maccabees 15: 37, 38.

5

Afterwards

She went back.

Work was completed on her South American journals for publication early in 1824, and as soon as the end of April she learned of the 'ill natured if not malicious'[1] review of the Brazil journal in the *Literary Gazette*, but was too busy seeing relatives and making preparations for her voyage to pay it much attention. In early July she set out, and after a passage of only thirty-three days reached Pernambuco.

John Murray, her publisher, received a letter written from Rio on 17 September 1824 in which Maria reported meeting Lord Cochrane at Pernambuco, '. . . blockading the place. He appeared in high health and spirits . . . meanwhile I have a fourth little princess of 6 weeks old, and all things seem to be increasing as well as the Imperial family.'[2] She had a charming apartment of seven rooms over the Empress's own, and had already become 'the best friends imaginable' with her royal pupil, the young Princess. The only fly in the ointment was that 'there are some expressions in my Brazil [journal] that have offended some of the English here, and I found a regular mutiny against me when I came.'[3] This disagreeable situation was improving however.

A curtain now descends on Maria's activities at the Imperial court of Brazil. Apart from indignant letters to John Murray concerning the unfriendly criticism of her Journals in the *Quarterly Review* and reiterations of support for Lord Cochrane, nothing is known as to why or when she left again for England, save for some dated sketches which show she remained in Brazil for a year. All that is certain is that by May 1826 she was back in London hard at work once more reading MSS for John Murray, writing articles and painstakingly editing someone else's ill-composed account of the Sandwich Islands. The next step came out of the blue.

> Poor Callcott is to marry the intrepid Mrs Graham [wrote Lady Holland apropos]. He is a quiet man, hitherto very happy with his own family, who live round him, and many who depend upon him entirely for subsistence. Unfortunately he fell in with this undaunted lady, and there he sank. It vexes all his friends, for she will quite sink him, being a most determined lady and as proud as Lucifer of her family and connections. Besides she has not a penny, probably debts, a bad prospect for him poor man. She is writing a history of Spain, so her pen and his brush are the *fond du ménage*.[4]

Augustus Callcott, gentle, humorous 'courteous and somewhat of a courtier'[5] was forty-seven, and a painter of soft and dreamlike landscapes that at the time were exceedingly popular. He lived in a pleasant *cul-de-sac* called The Mall, near Kensington Gravel Pits next to his brother's house, a rabbit warren of family life, much enjoyed by the bachelor uncle.

In the autumn of 1826 Maria moved to lodgings at 8 High Row, Kensington Gravel Pits, close therefore to The Mall where Augustus lived and painted. While here she obviously 'fell in' with the artist. He, in Lady Holland's words, appears to have 'sunk' almost immediately.

Six months later they were married. Three months after they set off on a protracted honeymoon to Europe.

This was rather less restful than it sounds, since for most of the time they travelled ceaselessly by steam-packet, private coach, (and once on a conveyance called an 'Eil-wagen') through Germany, Bavaria, Austria, Italy, France. They set out each day never later than seven in the morning, and usually at five. 'Not well – spitting blood,'[6] Maria noted from time to time, but drove on, ignoring her symptoms. The object of their travels seems to have been to comb the European picture galleries, and ransack book and print shops for treasures to bring back to Kensington, and into this Maria put all the energy and fervour which she had formerly laid out on Icelandic, Persian, Hindu Mythology. . . .

On 13 October having passed through a mountainous landscape 'savage even to horror', they crossed into Italy, which Maria already knew well, but which Augustus had never visited.

At Venice she revelled in Tintoretto's 'stormy brush', at Milan grieved over Leonardo's *Last Supper* '. . . worse, much worse than when I saw it 8 years ago – more faded in colour and more chipped . . .',[7] at Florence, where they arrived in dense fog, she bought a head reputedly by Botticelli.

By early January they were in Rome, where in spite of intermittent blisterings and blood-lettings she and Augustus amused themselves in the English artists' colony which, among scores of others, included Maria's old friend, Eastlake, Mrs Gaskell, Arthur Hallam, Keats's friend, Joseph Severn, and John Gibson the sculptor.

There followed thereafter, a five-day journey to Naples (during which their coach had to be dug out of a ploughed field), Pompeii, Amalfi, Naples, Rome (again), Siena, Florence (for the second time), Pisa, Genoa, Monaco, Nice, Paris, and, on 4 June 1828, Calais.

Mercifully, perhaps, they never again went abroad. Arrived back at Kensington, Maria at once set to work, this time on a translation from the French of a History of Turkey. Meanwhile her two-volume *History of Spain* was published and well reviewed, and she and Augustus took up again with their large circle of friends.

But two years later her life once more abruptly changed. A blood vessel suddenly rupturing left her so weakened that from now on she became a chronic invalid.

Like Coleridge in his lime-tree bower, she became a prisoner in the west-facing ground-floor room where

> A little bed was placed in a recess close to the window against which vines had been trained as natural blinds, and living arabesques were made among the shoots and branches by mice and birds, as they came, half tamed, to take the meats which Lady Callcott* daily placed for them; – a sort of pensioner bird, too feeble to sing or hop, was a constant companion and an object of her kind solicitude, and a noble hound was a privileged visitor at all times.[8]

Here she held court, appearing 'somewhat imperious' in her state chamber,[9] Augustus being more of a silent listener, as she entertained her friends, Sydney Smith, Thomas Campbell, the contentious Samuel Rogers, Maria Edgeworth, Harriet Martineau, Fanny Kemble, Caroline Fox.

Of these Caroline Fox was probably the closest. Eighteen years older than Maria she was the sister of the third Lord Holland, and a much-loved aunt at nearby Holland House. The two women had much in common. Both loved animals and flowers, were bookish, amused by politics, interested in education, with which Miss Fox's

* Augustus had been knighted by Queen Victoria.

unremitting philanthropic efforts among the poor children of Kensington and Shepherd's Bush were largely concerned.

At this time Maria had her own ideas about education, and about adult education in particular, which anticipated much later developments.

> Now indeed I build castles [she wrote]. I can imagine a village schoolroom, used, as Miss Austen somewhere says, for tormenting little children all day, open at night for the Welsh harper, the Irish piper, or the English glee-singer to instruct, for an hour or two, the grown-ups in their pleasant arts, and if a Scotch fiddler dropped in, and some did dance, and some drank tea provided by the school-master's wife, what harm?[10]

She and Miss Fox often corresponded more frivolously than this however; letters about personalities, Samuel Rogers in particular, who '*ordered* me never to *pollute* the name of Whig (*his* party!!!!!!) by calling myself one!';[11] letters from Maria's dog Lillo to Miss Fox's little dog Tiny; letters sometimes a thought too outspoken, 'I must write what is in my mind or nothing.'[12] Perhaps it is unsurprising that on her seventy-fifth birthday Caroline Fox recorded how much Maria had contributed to the enjoyment of her 'winter years of life'.

She continued to work. Her most famous book, *Little Arthur's History of England*, was published in 1835. 'I am going to put in the cake-toasting of Alfred,' she explained apropos to Miss Fox, 'and more-over make a little niche somewhere for King Arthur . . . I am making an experiment you know – not meaning to read any authorities till I see how my memory would serve to *tell* the history to an intelligent child. I shall *then* read and correct – maybe print.'[13]

The simple formula proved wonderfully successful, seventy editions within the next hundred years, nearly a million copies sold worldwide.

Over the next seven years other titles inexorably followed; *Essays towards a History of Painting, The Seven Ages of Shakespeare, The Little Brackenburners and Little Mary's four Sundays, A Scripture Herbal.* Finally, when she at last grew too weak to hold her pen she began to dictate her reminiscences to dear Miss Fox.

Strangely she had reached that very point where long before, at the age of twenty, she had first fallen ill. Now, in her green-shaded room, she evoked the Scottish scenery she had so much loved, the woods, lakes and waterfalls, the great castles and hospitable mansions she had visited, the whole marvellous opening of her intellectual life. 'I had discovered in my own mind powers of which

I had never even guessed the existence, and, perhaps not unhappily for me, I had been forced to practise forbearance and self-control to a degree that, while it fortified my moral character, and fitted me for the very hard life I have undergone, first broke down that robust health which I had always enjoyed, and brought to light the beginning of that disease of which I am now dying.'[14]

She continued dictating for a few pages more, speaking of that first convalescence, of reading during the following long winter, Gibbon's *Decline and Fall*, Burnett's *History of the Reformation*, Shakespeare, Milton, Corneille . . . then her attention dramatically switched, 'Another change', she caused her old friend to write, 'was now to take place in my life. . . .'[15]

They were the last words Miss Fox took down. On 21 November 1842 her friend died. She was fifty-seven.

'Noble, direct, generous, forgiving, quick, sensitive, kind sympathetic, and religious . . .'[16] listed the admiring obituary in the *Gentleman's Magazine*. All these things she had been!

In what she called a 'jingling doggerel' written as a contribution to a literary magazine run by some young nephews and nieces she had aptly summed up the circumstances of that last stage of her life.

> An old bureau – an elbow chair
> Of shape antique and fashion rare,
> Another of more modern cut,
> To which a swinging desk is put.
> Three tables of three different sizes,
> Three seats so stuffed they're sought as prizes
> By all who come on weary legs
> To view what's hanging on the pegs,
> To right, to left – behind, before,
> Above the fire, upon the door.
> No corner lost – but here a gem,
> Or picture – there a print, and mem.
> Two of 'em are but immature.
> Then gold-ground saints of face demure
> From Pisa – more than half a score.
> One standing and one swinging screen,
> Two marble vases, and between
> Them stands an Indian cup,
> From which we mattee used to sup
> Through slender tubes – then Wedgwood's vases
> For holding flowers – letter-cases,
> And baskets, boxes, drawers all crammed,
> Then books and bookcases all jammed

Close into corners, where they hold
More tongues than Babel ever told.
Then there's a large white dog called Lillo,
Who makes his master's foot his pillow;
A sleek black cat who mews and purrs,
And with her sables shames our furs.
A grate adorned with Roman fasces;
Two cherubs' heads maintain their places
On either side – and right before 'em
A table stands in due decorum.
Beyond, an arch sustains the ceiling;
On either side with tasteful feeling
Hang carv'd wreaths, a Surzana hat,
A modelled gem; and over that
Are everlastings, to denote
How long its fame may keep afloat.
But here our book must have an end,
And so 'Goodbye, dear reader-friend.'[17]

Sources

Books by Maria Graham

Journal of a residence in India, Constable, Edinburgh 1812.
Three months passed in the mountains east of Rome during the year 1819, Longman, London 1820.
Journal of a voyage to Brazil and residence there during 1821–1823,* Longman & John Murray, London 1824.
Journal of a residence in Chile during 1822,† Longman & John Murray, London 1824.

Biography
Rosamund Brunel Gotch, *Maria Callcott, the creator of 'Little Arthur'*,‡, John Murray, London 1937. This is the only biography of Maria Graham and is, in its slightly old-fashioned way, excellent, since it is based on hitherto unpublished diaries and family papers.

Abbreviations

* *Brazil* in Notes.
† *Chile* in Notes.
‡ Gotch in Notes.

Notes

Introduction

1. *Chile*, p. 326.
2. Ibid., p. 299.
3. Ibid., p. 145.
4. The Earl of Ilchester (ed.), *Journal of the Hon. Henry Edward Fox, 4th Lord Holland*, 1923, p. 272.
5. Gotch, p. 244.
6. Ibid., p. 245.

1 Beginnings

1. Gotch, note p. 25.
2. Ibid., p. 32.
3. Ibid., p. 36.
4. Ibid., p. 39.
5. Ibid.
6. Ibid., p. 48.
7. Ibid., p. 63.
8. Ibid., p. 75.
9. Ibid., p. 130.
10. Ibid., p. 132.
11. Ibid., p. 140.
12. Ibid., p. 141.
13. Ibid., p. 144.
14. Ibid., p. 150.
15. Ibid., p. 154.
16. Ibid.
17. Ibid., p. 156.
18. Ibid., p. 183.
19. The Rev. William Mavor, *Universal History*, 1810, Vol. 24, p. 198.

2 Brazil Journal

10 January – 20 April 1822
1. Brazil, p. 192.
2. Ibid., p. 207.
3. Ibid.
4. Ibid.

3 Chile Journal

28 April – 12 June 1822
1. *Chile*, p. 148.

19 June – 24 August 1822
1. *Chile*, p. 186.
2. Ibid., p. 188.
3. Ibid., p. 194.
4. Ibid., p. 195.

25 August – 7 September 1822
1. *Chile*, p. 213.
2. Ibid., p. 221.

8 September – 24 September 1822
1. *Chile*, p. 241.
2. Ibid., p. 242.
3. Ibid., p. 248.
4. Ibid., p. 253.
5. Ibid., p. 254.
6. Ibid., p. 259.

20 November 1822 – 18 January 1823
1. *Chile*, p. 304.
2. Ibid., p. 315.
3. Ibid., p. 316.

4. Ibid., p. 333.
5. Ibid., p. 334.
6. Ibid., p. 335.
7. Ibid., p. 340.
8. Ibid., p. 341.
9. Ibid.
10. Ibid., p. 342.

4 Brazil Journal 2

19 June – 15 August 1823
1. *Brazil*, p. 259.

5 Afterwards
1. Gotch, p. 243.
2. Ibid.
3. Ibid., p. 244.
4. The Earl of Ilchester,
   Chronicles of Holland House,
   p. 106.

5. Gotch, p. 255.
6. Ibid., p. 256.
7. Ibid., p. 263.
8. *Gentleman's Magazine* 1843,
   Part 1, p. 98.
9. The Earl of Ilchester,
   Chronicles of Holland House,
   p. 46.
10. Gotch, p. 287.
11. Ibid., p. 297.
12. Ibid., p. 289.
13. Ibid., p. 85.
14. Ibid.
15. Ibid., p. 301.
16. *Gentleman's Magazine*, 1843,
   Part 1, p. 98..
17. Gotch, p. 301.

Index